# Has Anyone Seen My Pants?

# Has Anyone Seen My Pants?

## SARAH COLONNA

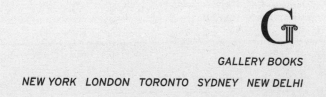

**GALLERY BOOKS**

*NEW YORK LONDON TORONTO SYDNEY NEW DELHI*

GALLERY BOOKS

A Division of Simon & Schuster, Inc.

1230 Avenue of the Americas

New York, NY 10020

First Gallery Books trade paperback edition March 2015

GALLERY BOOKS and colophon are registered trademarks of Simon & Schuster, Inc.

For information about special discounts for bulk purchases, please contact Simon & Schuster Special Sales at 1-866-506-1949 or business@simonandschuster.com.

The Simon & Schuster Speakers Bureau can bring authors to your live event. For more information or to book an event contact the Simon & Schuster Speakers Bureau at 1-866-248-3049 or visit our website at www.simonspeakers.com.

Interior design by Jaime Putorti
Cover design by John Vairo Jr.
Cover photography by Blake Little

Manufactured in the United States of America

10 9 8 7 6 5 4 3 2 1

Library of Congress Cataloging-in-Publication Data

Colonna, Sarah, 1974–
  Has anyone seen my pants? / Sarah Colonna.
     pages cm
  1. Colonna, Sarah, 1974– 2. Women comedians—United States—Biography.
  3. Television actors and actresses—United States—Biography. 4. Television comedy
  writers—United States—Biography. I. Title.
   PN2287.C5745A3 2015
   818'.602—dc23
                                    2014039354

ISBN 978-1-4767-7192-2
ISBN 978-1-4767-7193-9 (ebook)

To Jon. Thank you for changing how it ends . . .

I'm a *train* wreck, I'm a mess

But I'm gonna take you dancing

Put on your party dress

—RHETT MILLER, OLD 97'S

## *Prologue*

It's midnight and I'm under a pile of covers, writing this from my bed with a pillow propping up my laptop. I have the heat cranked up to seventy-five degrees because it's currently "winter" in Southern California, which means it's about fifty degrees outside, a temperature I now consider "freezing." I grew up in a state that has real winters, but my seventeen years in California have weakened me to the elements and I am *not* ashamed of it. It's called "adapting," assholes.

I'm single, which is probably pretty obvious from the above description. If I were married or in a serious adult relationship, someone would share this bed with me and my late-night typing and cranked-up heater would no doubt be an issue. Also, I have hardwood floors and often hear noises at night. I used to think the noises were just my cat walking around upstairs, but now that he's dead, I've ruled him out. The condo I live in is wonderful but older, so maybe that line my mom used to feed me when I was younger and too terrified to sleep about how our house was "settling" was true all along and that's what's going on here. At least that's what I tell myself when I'm trying to get back to sleep and am out of temazepam. I've already gone upstairs to check for burglars and ghosts. *Yes*, I've seen horror movies and I know everyone says you should just stay downstairs, but why lie here and wait to be killed when I can go upstairs with my signed Mark Trumbo baseball bat and get killed a little faster?

I'm not complaining about living alone. I've resided here by myself for a few years now, after an attempt at living with a boyfriend ended in . . . well, my living alone. And before that I lived roommate-free for seven years. So, aside from the lack of sleep because I hear my dead cat's footsteps on the wooden staircase in the middle of the night, I really enjoy being the solo master of the house (well, condo).

I'm a big fan of alone time, I'm a big fan of silence, and I'm a big fan of getting to do whatever I want—and of knowing nobody is putting my expensive underwear in the fucking dryer. That said, I think my joy in being alone might be a little bit of a problem; I'm not sure how the hell I'm ever going to manage to share my space with anyone ever again.

But all of that doesn't mean I don't want to have a real relationship or even get married someday. Yes, I'd like to get married someday. Most of the women I grew up with back in Arkansas would scoff at this, thinking I'm an old maid now and that ship has sailed. To that I say: Suck it. I chose a different path and I didn't judge you for getting married at sixteen. But if I hear you talk shit about me, all bets are off.

It was pretty easy to find a boyfriend or a date when my source of income was bartending. And it was *really* easy to find a one-night stand . . . I mean, after all, I was the *bartender*; I had all the power and all the booze.

But now I'm in my late thirties and have a real(ish) job, and that seems to be working against me; at least, this is what I assume . . . I mean, I can't imagine that *nobody on earth* is interested in me at all. Right? Hello?

I've definitely gotten a little better looking with age. A crazy English woman I worked with when I was twenty-four told me that this would happen because I'm a Capricorn, and she claimed that Capricorns are known to get better looking with age. So maybe she turned out to be right (hey—crazy people can be right sometimes, too). *Or,* maybe I've wised up since my early twenties, when I thought Slim Jims and Dr Pepper were nutritionally solid breakfast choices. Now I even eat kale sometimes and I've liked it one out of three of those times. How do you like me now, Arkansas?

I mean, I had boyfriends left and right in my twenties and at that point I had an unfortunate haircut, a terrible sense of fashion, and had never even considered getting a bikini wax. *You wanna put hot wax* WHERE? *I don't think so, big German lady.*

But now I have pretty amazing hair. (It's okay to love your own hair. It's not like I made it myself or anything; I'm just grateful to my mother and father for having a sperm-egg mixture that created this glorious mane.) I dress decently for someone with very little sense of style and my bikini area is properly maintained at all times, even in the winter. *You need me, naked from the waist down, to pull my knees into my chest so you can get "back there"?* No problem, *petite Asian lady.* (I like to think of it as a form of yoga: Scared Naked Baby Pose.)

The fact that a man would be bothered by dating someone who is doing pretty well for herself doesn't make a ton of sense to me; most of my male friends joke that they would love to have a woman who paid for everything while they just planned golf outings. But I don't think that's exactly what I'm looking for, or I guess I'd be dating one of my male friends.

So what am I looking for? That's the million-dollar question. What I *do* know, is that most of all, I'm looking for someone who loves to order appetizers. Anyone who doesn't is a terrorist.

It isn't easy to find balance in life. You finally get one thing nailed down and another thing falls off the wall because the nail wasn't strong enough to keep it up there. Or maybe the nail was strong enough but got tired of holding the other piece up and didn't want to have to do all the work anymore. NOT THAT I'VE EVER FELT THAT WAY OR ANYTHING.

When most aspects of your life are functioning pretty well

as they are, does it mean that the one missing aspect, be it work, family, or a significant other, can never be fulfilled? Or do I just need a hobby or something? Sheesh, apparently all this alone time makes me ponder life's bigger mysteries.

Oops, be right back, I just heard something moving around upstairs . . .

## Recycle, Reduce, Reuse

At age thirty-five, I became single after a five-year relationship that included a failed attempt at living with a man romantically for the first time in my life.

I guess I didn't realize that when you move in with someone, they're there *all the time.* I'd come home from work and Ryan would just be there, lurking around. He had to remind me time after time that this was because he lived there. But I'd had roommates in the past, and occasionally they would leave the house. What was it with this guy? Seriously, I almost called the police on him once just to get him out for the evening. That's not a great sign.

And as much as I assured myself I'd never be in a sexless relationship, eventually that's what ours became. Ryan was always judging me for *everything*—my taste in music was stupid, my laugh was too loud, and if I wanted to crack open a bottle of wine after a long day of work, I had a problem. For someone who claimed to love me, he certainly didn't appear to like me. That stuff really wears on a person, so we inevitably became a cliché: I was turned off by the fact that he thought the dryer was a drawer, and he was turned off by the fact that I was turned off. Look, I'm sure moving in with the *right* person can be a lovely experience, but although he and I had some good times and a few successful "game nights" (I believe those were invented by a couple in the late 1940s who could no longer stand being alone in the same room on Tuesday evenings), it turns out we weren't a good match, so living together was much less fun than, well, *not* living together.

Since I knew I didn't want to date anybody that I worked with and wasn't interested in meeting guys at bars, I did what any well-adjusted single woman in her mid-thirties who doesn't have a lot of time to meet new people would do—I recycled an ex-lover. This may not seem like the best idea, but as far as I could tell the pros outweighed the cons: you know, the time-honored tradition of "he's already seen me naked so technically I'm not adding another number to my roster."

I homed in on one particular ex, Patrick, because he had always checked in on me over the years, through mutual friends, to find out whether or not I was single. Our previous relationship was short-lived due to the fact he was a raging alcoholic and because of his love for strippers (he lived near a strip club and often allowed the girls to come over to his place and "use his shower," claiming he had great water pressure, which was handy when removing pesky glitter). Years later, he seemed to fancy me "the one that got away" and I liked the idea of spending my newfound singledom with someone who romanticized me. Plus, like many alcoholics, he was a blast to hang out with.

As I suspected, Patrick was very excited to find out that I was single. He told me he wanted to take me on a date, so I made all the usual manicure/pedicure/bikini wax appointments one makes when trying to impress someone, bought a new top, put on my best "ass jeans," and headed over to his place. (He couldn't pick me up because his license was temporarily suspended due to a couple of DUI arrests. Thinking back, I probably didn't need to get a new top for the date . . .)

When he answered the door, I remembered why I used to like him so much; he was a few years older than me but had this boyish charm that made my stomach jump. He made me a drink while we waited for a taxi to take us to his favorite local restaurant/wine bar. Even though we hadn't seen each other in a few years, everything felt easy—conversation was easy, laughing was easy; it all came naturally. That also reminded me why I used to like him so much—we just clicked. The only hiccup of the evening (besides his) was when we got to the restaurant and he took off his jacket to reveal a T-shirt that said "I Love Bacon."

"Really?" I asked as I nodded toward his shirt.

"What? I love bacon, it's not like I'm wearing a lie."

"Fair enough," I laughed. *So he's a forty-year-old man wearing a T-shirt that says "I Love Bacon,"* I thought. *I suppose I've dated worse, but, damn it, I* really *wish I hadn't spent one penny on a new top.*

The night continued as expected: we both got really drunk and went back to his place to have sex. Granted this was not the most romantic evening in history, but the relationship I'd just ended had taken a while to get out of, and now I felt so free and so happy to be hanging out with someone who wasn't constantly rolling his eyes at me like Ryan always had. I just wanted to have fun, and Patrick the alcoholic was a lot of fun.

We started hanging out pretty often, usually at bars, but ours was a summer fling and since we both loved baseball, we also went to a lot of games (Patrick really liked day games because it gave him an excuse to drink beer at noon). When we dated before, he owned a bar/restaurant but now was unemployed, which meant he was always available for good times. I don't want you to think I was dating a loser with no job, though. Patrick had sold his bar, plus he had inherited a large sum of money when his father passed away, so essentially I was dating a loser with no job but *with* money—hey, at least I wasn't paying for everything.

Lots of money and no job probably sounds great to some people, but it comes with issues. Having that kind of money and that kind of time on your hands can lead to really poor decisions, especially if you already have an addictive personality like Patrick had. But he lived close to my work, so I often spent the night at his house (he had his own house!), and there was lots and lots of humping. Holy shit, I did not realize how pent up I was from the last six months of my previous relationship, in which there was no humping. So I was trying to get into Patrick's pants every chance I could.

Now, most men would have been stoked that the girl he was dating always wanted sex, but Patrick wasn't normal. I mean, he was up for it a lot of the time, but definitely not as often as I wanted. One day when I asked him why he didn't want to have sex with me—I mean, hello, I was wearing a dress and heels—he explained that unlike my previous relationship, his previous relationship had not been sexless . . .

"She used to get other girls, friends of hers, to come over and join us," he explained nonchalantly.

"Huh?" I asked as I drained the drink in my hand.

"She was kind of a mess, Sarah. I met her on this website and—"

"I assume you don't mean ChristianMingle?"

"Ha ha, very funny. No, it was a website where girls who want to date men with money put up profiles."

*"You met her on a sugar-daddy website? That's where you met your ex-girlfriend?"* I was talking loudly. That's what I do sometimes when people say stupid things. But truthfully, I wasn't that shocked. I'd known Patrick for years and even when we were just friends, when the girls weren't over at his place "showering," he was at the strip club, often handing over wads of cash to go into the back room—which I don't think is used for playing pinochle—with the dancers. (I never said I was proud of this particular recycle, so just bear with me.)

"You asked me a question; I'm just being honest with you," he said, very matter-of-fact.

He was right; I had asked. Now I sort of wish I hadn't, but I took a deep breath, apologized, and allowed him to continue on with his super-fucked-up story. He told me all about his ex-girlfriend, their "interesting" sex, and her meth problem.

*"She did meth?"*

"Sarah . . ."

"Sorry, I meant"—(whispering)—"she did meth?"

"Yeah, she was a mess. And after we broke up I let her live in my guesthouse because I felt bad for her; she didn't have any other place to go. But she ended up stealing from me and when I confronted her about it she called the police and tried to have *me* arrested."

"For what? For not wanting to be stolen from? That seems like a weird charge."

"She told them I hit her."

*"You hit her?"*

"Of course not, I'd never—"

"I know, I'm sorry." I did know. Patrick wasn't a violent drunk. He was more of a "sing karaoke until most of the bar clears out because you keep taking the mic out of other people's hands"–type drunk. He'd clearly gotten involved with one of those girls he paid extra to go in a back room with and experienced what it was like to try to take the stripper out of the girl. Plus, who would make that shit up? It wasn't exactly a turn-on. But apparently she had been so sex crazed that my pulling on his belt every ten seconds wasn't exactly what he was looking for this time around. *Great timing.*

Now, you'd think that all of that information, along with his alcoholism and employment situation, would have made me stop seeing Patrick, but you would be incorrect. He had several great qualities. First of all, he had a good heart. I knew him well and I knew (or at least believed) that his penchant for women such as strippers came from a place of wanting to help them. I'm not saying it was smart—his brain was rarely operating at full speed—but I always thought his heart was in the right place. Second, and most important, he let me blast country music in his house at two o'clock in the morning. My ex hated country music! He never let me play country music! *Fuck him!* So I decided that Patrick allowing me to play it was more important than any potential red flags. And, yes, I had "feelings" for him and his rugged features. It's like the old saying: the heart wants what the vagina wants.

At some point, Patrick became involved in horse racing. It seemed to come out of nowhere, but he also seemed to take it very seriously. (You know, the whole "too much time on his hands" thing: Money + Time = Poor Decisions.) I also started to notice his odd sleeping habits, like when I'd wake up at four a.m. and find him in the living room on his laptop buying old typewriters.

"Why do you need an old typewriter?"

"I buy them and resell them," he explained, as if I was the asshole.

"Okay," I said, and went back to bed, not wanting to engage in a conversation about typewriters because . . . well, who does?

I'd go to work and wouldn't hear from him all day, because that was apparently when he slept. One evening after work, I swung by his house to pick up a jacket I had left and found that he was in bed at six o'clock in the evening. That would have been no big deal if he was just taking a nap, but he hadn't been up yet at all that day. I felt myself judging him and tried to shake it off: I was *not* going to be like Ryan, I was going to let Patrick be Patrick.

"So I like to sleep during the day, what's the big deal?" he asked.

"I don't know, just . . . shouldn't you be doing something else?"

"Like what?"

"I don't know . . . anything else!" It was quickly becoming impossible for me not to feel like I was judging his lifestyle, but I work long hours and when I get off work I work on other stuff. Yes, I enjoy my cocktails and make time for fun, but I feel like I earn my fun time because of all the work time. He was just on constant fun time, which was starting to be no fun to me.

Right around the time the obvious cracks in this rebound were starting to shine through, Ryan (the ex I had just broken up with) started contacting me. Go figure, right? Isn't that how it always works?

Ryan missed me and was sorry that he didn't "appreciate" me the way he "should have," and blah blah blah. It was all so cliché that it embarrassed me for him a little bit. I mean, I know he really believed—now that I was gone—that he couldn't live without me, but I also knew that if we got back together things would go right back to the way they were before. I was finally comfortable with myself and I wasn't willing to go back to someone who wasn't. Also, I just wasn't in love with him anymore.

Ryan told me that he had changed, that he knew he made me feel judged and cornered, and that he wouldn't do that to me again. He said he was unhappy with his own life so he took it out on me. I knew that all of this was true, but unfortunately his realizing it now didn't make me fall in love with him again. The end of our relationship had dragged on for months while we tried to "figure it out," but what happens in that case, especially for the person who really knows it's over, is that you let go of it during that time, so when it does officially end, you're already through the grieving process and on to the "I can't wait to hump somebody else" process. Ryan was just now in his grieving process and it wasn't pretty.

Since I had loved him for a long time, it hurt me to know he was in pain. But giving him any false hope was definitely not the answer. So with each e-mail or text, I responded by gently telling him that I knew we weren't right for each other, that soon he'd know it, too, and that he was just missing me right now.

"But I'm a completely different man now," he wrote to me in one forty-seven-page e-mail. "I went on a yoga retreat and it changed me. I'm a vegan now."

The fact he was now into yoga and veganism just drove the whole "we aren't right for each other" thing home for me.

"I ate a cheeseburger for breakfast," I wrote back, still trying to tell him gently that getting back together wasn't going to happen. I didn't want to have to write the words "I don't love you anymore" to him. Maybe I should have, maybe the harsh truth was the better way to go, but I didn't want to hurt him again. I just wanted him to move on.

Meanwhile, in an effort to restoke the dying flame between us, Patrick and I decided to go to Catalina Island for a weekend. It's only a short ferry ride away from L.A., but Catalina kind of makes you feel like you actually went somewhere. There isn't a ton to do unless you're into riding ATVs or hiking, so we just headed straight to a bar and did one of our mutual favorite things: weekend day drinking.

Day drinking turned into night drinking, which led to our throwing popcorn at each other in our hotel room and passing out. You know—romance. We woke up the next morning, politely cleaned all of the popcorn out of the bed so that housekeeping didn't think we were animals, and went back out to start day drinking again until the ferry came later that afternoon. It was a successful weekend in that we had a lot of laughs, but in the back of my mind all I could think was that he could do this all the time if he wanted to, like constantly—not only because he had no job, but worse, because he had no ambition. And that, I realized as I sat watching him suck down a Bloody Mary on the ferry ride back home and back to reality, was the real problem. But it was a problem I wasn't quite ready to face just yet.

A couple of days after we got back from Catalina Island, I sold a TV show based on my first book. This, obviously, was a very big deal to me. It's not an easy thing to do, selling a show, and it was a dream of mine. Now, it's not like there's a guarantee that the show you sell is going to end up on television, but it's one of many steps and it's definitely one worth celebrating. So, I decided that Patrick and I, along with my friend Jackie and her boyfriend, Brandon, needed to go out and do just that.

I told Patrick to be at my house at seven p.m.; I had ordered a car to pick us up shortly after. I was going all out for this. I was even wearing a new dress; so was Jackie. This was a big night for me and she knew it. So when Patrick arrived around seven forty-five p.m. wearing a T-shirt that said "Who Farted?" I stared at him in disbelief.

"What?" he asked, completely clueless. "I didn't know we were dressing up!"

"You didn't have to dress up, you could have just not worn that!" I said, almost in tears. "What are you, in some kind of Dumb T-shirt of the Month Club or something?"

"It's just a T-shirt," he responded, still clueless.

He was right, it was just a T-shirt—a T-shirt that said "Who Farted?" on it, and he was a forty-year-old man. I suddenly found myself longing for another "I Love Bacon" T-shirt.

"Do you want him to wear Brandon's shirt?" Jackie asked, referring to her boyfriend, who was wearing a nice button-down shirt like a normal adult male.

"Wait, then what will I wear?" Brandon asked in a panic.

"I guess the 'Who Farted?' shirt," Jackie answered, clearly not having thought things through.

"No, no," I interrupted. "Brandon isn't going to have to go out in public in that shirt just because Patrick is a moron."

"I'm right here," Patrick said.

"Yeah. You're right here. *Wearing a T-shirt that says 'Who Farted?' on it and we're going to a nice restaurant.* So, guess what? You don't get to be offended right now."

"Jesus, what's the big deal?" he asked, dead serious.

"The big deal is: it's Sarah's night, a special night, and you showed up wearing something her thirteen-year-old nephew wouldn't even wear," Jackie said, her voice raised.

"Her nephew would *love* this shirt," Patrick snapped back.

"*That's* your defense?" I asked.

"Look, I'm sorry. Jesus. I'll wear my jacket and I won't unzip it. Okay?" he said, relenting.

"Whatever, yes. Fine," I said. The car had now been waiting for us for close to an hour and I just wanted to get to the restaurant and order a giant martini. "But if you unzip it even for a second I'll kill you. Like even if your jacket catches on fire you can't take it off—you just have to sit in it and burn to death. And you'll deserve to."

We finally made it to the restaurant and Patrick kept his jacket zipped as promised. But throughout dinner he kept looking at his phone, which I hate. I know we all spend too much time on our phones now, but when you're out to dinner, unless you're waiting for an important phone call from your family or your job—which Patrick was not—put your fucking phone away.

"Why do you keep looking at your phone?" I asked him while Jackie and Brandon stepped outside to have a cigarette.

"What? I don't."

"Yes you do. Constantly. It's rude."

"What is with you tonight?" he asked me.

"What is with *me* tonight? With *me*?"

"Oh, here we go . . . ," Patrick said in the world's most condescending tone.

"Yeah, here we go," I repeated. "Here's what is *with me*, you asshole: Tonight was important to me. I have been busting my ass for years and selling this show is a huge deal and I wanted to celebrate with people I care about, but one of them showed up forty-five minutes late wearing a wacky T-shirt and has been texting God knows who during the entire meal."

"You were much easier to get along with when you were just a bartender," Patrick replied.

I was stunned. But at the same time, I wasn't. Things were different this time around for us. It didn't work out the first time, but that was more because he wasn't ready to settle down and be in a relationship and I was. This time the problem was that I'd grown up and he hadn't.

When the night ended, Patrick came home with me. He was hammered, of course, so when we walked in the door, he immediately passed out. I put on eight layers of pajamas because I didn't want him to wake up and think I wanted to have sex with him. I pretty much hated him at this point, and I knew with all the alcohol he'd consumed he'd never have the energy to get that many pairs of bottoms off of me. When I crawled into bed, I noticed his phone lying out on the nightstand. It was beckoning me.

I know, I *know*. "If you go looking for something, you'll find it," or "Don't go looking for something if you don't want to find it," or whatever that saying is that guilty people who have shit to hide always say . . . I *know*. But he had been acting really weird all night on that phone and the last thing in the world he would ever do was be honest with me. So, if I wanted to know what he was up to, I was going to have to find out for myself.

He was texting his slutty, meth-addicted ex-girlfriend. So, if you still have any problem with my going through his phone, I'm right and you're wrong.

I shook him awake, hard. When he woke up, I was sweating either out of anger, or because I was wearing eight layers of clothes.

"What the fuck? Why did you wake me up? And why are you so sweaty?"

"So you were texting *her*? That's what you were doing all night . . . on *my* night? My night to celebrate? Texting a whore?"

"You went through my—"

"Save it. Yes, I went through your phone. In the future, if you don't want someone to do that, don't make your passcode your fucking birth date. Seriously, even your passcode is an idiot."

"It isn't what you think . . ." Patrick started to defend himself.

"What do I think? Huh? Tell me what I think."

"Are you wearing multiple pairs of pajamas?"

"Stop trying to distract me. Why were you texting her? You told her you'd meet her at your house tomorrow afternoon. *Why?*"

"Like I said, it isn't what you—"

"Just answer the fucking question!"

"I'm trying to, but you keep interrupting me."

He had a point. But I was fuming.

"Fine, go ahead. Tell me why you were meeting her tomorrow."

"You know how I'm leaving in two days for New Jersey? And you know how I have that huge fear of flying? Well, she has Xanax. She always has Xanax, and I need some to get through the flight."

"She also always has meth," I retorted. I did know he was going back home to New Jersey for the weekend and I did know he had a huge fear of flying. But *come on.*

"Sarah, I swear to you, I wasn't going to do anything with her. She was going to drop off the Xanax and that was it."

Even if he was telling the truth, it didn't matter. This is a woman who stole from him and then filed false charges against him. I don't care if she shits Xanax—she wasn't someone he should have been talking to. And that's when it hit me: I didn't want him talking to her, but he didn't mind talking to her. He didn't mind that she was basically a prostitute who had trashed his life for a significant amount of time. He still needed someone to save.

"Patrick, you know who else has Xanax? Doctors. You can go tell a doctor about your flying problem and they'll write you a big fat prescription for Xanax. Trust me, I've done it and I'm not even afraid of flying—I just really like Xanax."

"Yeah, but then I would have had to make an appointment and go to a doctor—"

"You have time to go to the doctor! You have more time than anybody in the world to go to the doctor. In fact, you have time to go to the doctor on behalf of everybody in the world!"

"What does that mean?" he asked.

I was too exhausted to explain anything to him. "It means this is over. That's what it means," I said, and I meant it.

"Wait, so you don't want to see me anymore just because I needed to get some Xanax?"

"If that's the story you have to tell yourself, then yes. This whole thing is over because you needed a Xanax." And with that, I kicked him out and never spoke to him again.

I had so much more to say but I knew it would fall on deaf ears. The truth was, I didn't want people like his ex-girlfriend in my life. And if I were with him, by default, she'd be in my life. I think if someone steals from you, then tries to get you thrown in jail, they aren't really a fun hang, but maybe that's just me. At the end of the day, his texting her or not wasn't even the real problem. The problem was that Patrick was stuck at the maturity level of a twenty-one-year-old. He just wanted to drink, sleep, and repeat. Our relationship was certainly a nice distraction for me after coming out of a relationship that had ceased to know the meaning of fun for so many months. But when it started to distract me from what was important, the fun ended there. Relationship-wise, I had gone from one extreme to the other and I was pretty sure what I really wanted lay somewhere in the middle.

So that was that. I had rebounded right into another relationship and now that was over and I was finally really, truly single. After he left, I sat on my bed and tried to cry but the tears just wouldn't come.

*Why am I not sad?* I wondered. *Shouldn't I feel sad?*

I popped in *The Notebook,* which always makes me cry, even when I'm deliriously happy. But still the tears wouldn't come. Instead, every time Ryan Gosling came on the screen I just got super horny.

The next morning, I woke up to find a bag of some of my favorite things from Whole Foods on my doorstep with a note from Ryan (my ex, not Gosling), telling me he knew I was really busy and he hoped I was taking care of myself. I know it sounds like a lovely gesture, and it would have been about eighteen months before, but now it was just annoying. *Why are the guys I date all so annoying?*

"Did you get my gift?" a text from Ryan asked me about a half hour later.

"Yes. Thank you, that was really thoughtful," I lied.

"I just know you're so busy, I hope you're taking care of yourself."

"Yeah, that's what your note said," I responded.

"Ouch," he replied, and then went silent.

Two days later I got a text from him asking me to meet him for coffee. I was getting tired of saying no but I still didn't want to say yes.

"I'm sorry," I wrote back. "I just don't think it's a good idea."

"It's just coffee, Sarah."

"Is it?"

"I promise. Just coffee."

"And you won't talk about getting back together or anything like that?"

"I promise."

"And you won't send me an e-mail two hours later saying we should get back together or anything like that either?"

"I promise. Just coffee. I just want to see you and catch up. That's all."

I decided to go have coffee with him. Maybe he needed this. Maybe this would make him stop romanticizing our dead relationship.

We met at a bar by my house that fancies itself a tavern. Ryan ordered a light beer and some sort of quinoa salad. I ordered a margarita and a steak that I didn't even really want, in hopes that since he was a vegan now he'd be turned off by my meat-eating ways.

Much to my surprise, we had a pleasant time. There were no sparks, no regrets, and no mushy feelings. We just talked and it was fine and I even remembered why we used to be such good friends. He talked about how he went skydiving and how I should try it, and I talked about how I never ever wanted to go skydiving and how I hate it when people that have gone skydiving try to tell other people they should go.

"Planes are for staying inside of when they're in the air," I explained.

Then he showed me a picture of him mid-skydive—not a good look for anyone's face.

*We are so not right for each other*, I mused happily.

On my way home, I thought about how glad I was that I met him that afternoon and how it seemed like maybe we would be able to be friends down the road. I felt good.

That is, until about two hours later when I got an e-mail from Ryan. Remember a few paragraphs ago when he promised not to do this? Well, it turns out I was the only one who didn't feel regrets during our afternoon together.

His e-mail was sweet, thoughtful, and completely enraging. He posed a "hypothetical": What if I'd wandered into that bar today and met him but we had never met before? Would I have given him my number? Would I be willing to go out on a date with this "stranger" I'd just had a nice conversation with?

I'm sure some of you reading this think that sounds really romantic and you think I should've e-mailed him back and given this "stranger" one more shot. But you're wrong. We weren't strangers and this wasn't a rom-com starring Julia Roberts and whichever English actor you want to place in the other role.

See, his pleas didn't make me feel bad this time—they just pissed me off. During the five years we were together, I stood by him after he broke up with me and got back together with an ex-girlfriend he was hung up on—more than once. I flew to the East Coast multiple times to hang out with his family, one time at an *indoor water park* (gross). I went skiing with him one Christmas and I fucking hate skiing; I prefer the ocean. I don't want any of that snow nonsense when I'm trying to relax. In those five years, he came home to Arkansas with me one time and we never once went on a beach vacation. What I'm saying is: I tried. I put my time in. I was done. We didn't work.

And now that I had finally really walked away from him, I was happy and he wasn't. But it wasn't fair of him to keep hounding me and it certainly wasn't up to me to make him feel better about the fact that he'd lost me. I really, really wanted to tell him to fuck off. I wanted to scream, "I don't love you anymore! Is that what you need to hear?" at the top of my lungs. But I didn't have that in me, because I did love him once. So instead I said something along the lines of:

"I'm just not there. I'm sorry. I know you've made a lot of changes in your life for the positive, and I'm happy for you. I don't think we're a healthy combination as a couple. We don't fit; we've tried many times. I don't want you to take steps backward, and I don't want to either."

See, I'm not a complete asshole. As I pushed "send" on the e-mail to him, I knew I had finally closed that door. I felt I'd gotten my point across and I was proud of myself, because honestly, after the experience I'd just had dating Patrick the Drunk, the easy thing to do would have been to run back into Ryan's arms and just be with him forever. But if there's one thing I've learned, it's that things worth having don't always come easy. I looked around at the things in my life that were good, and they were all things I worked hard for and, more important, things I refused to settle for.

Lesson learned. Digging through the recycling bin is dangerous: if you grab the wrong object, you might end up with a giant piece of glass sticking right through your hand.

## Table for ¿Uno?

When you're single, the older you get, the more difficult it is to find someone to take a vacation with you. By now a lot of my friends are married, have kids, or both. The friends who have boyfriends are also more difficult to wrangle since most couples tend to vacation together. And for some reason not all of my friends' boyfriends are pumped about their girlfriends going to Mexico with me—as if my life is an Afterschool Special and I'm the bully peer pressuring everyone to act badly.

Last spring I really wanted to go to Mexico, so I convinced my friend Jackie, who is engaged, to go with me. Her fiancé didn't mind; I get along really well with him, plus she and I have been friends for like fifteen years or something. In fact, she's one of the people I went on vacation with when I was with my ex and *she* was single. So technically she owed me one.

We settled on Cabo San Lucas, which is totally unoriginal, but why fix what isn't broken? I found this amazing resort that had a five-night minimum and she was only able to go for four. But the resort looked so perfect that I figured I'd go one night ahead of her and do some writing.

I arrived in Cabo midday and had scheduled a car to pick me up. That sounds fancy, but if you've ever taken a taxi in Mexico, you know why I chose to book a town car. Miraculously, my driver was on time and I was quickly on my way to the lovely resort—vacation mode was setting in. Then the driver started talking. *What was I doing in Cabo? Where was I from? Was I meeting my husband?*

"No, I'm not married," I replied, kind of annoyed. Does every woman always have to be meeting her husband?

"Oh, so you meet your boyfren then?" he said, persisting in broken English.

"No, I'm meeting a friend."

"A girl?"

"Yeah, a girl. Can we stop talking? Sorry, I have a headache," I lied.

The driver ignored my request and continued with his interrogation: "You and you fren lesbian?"

"What? *No!*"

"Sorry I jus asking, I mean, you have no boyfren . . ."

"Some people are just . . . single. In America, anyway." Why was this guy trying to ruin my vacation already? PS: this wasn't the first time I'd been through this line of questioning in Mexico. "How old are you?" I asked.

"Twenty-two," he replied.

"And you're married?"

"Sí, we haf four kid." He smiled.

"Exactly," I replied, my point driven home to nobody but myself.

Luckily, just about then we pulled up to the resort. I handed him a twenty and got the fuck out of the car.

"Have fun with you 'fren,'" he yelled to me, using air quotes when he said "fren."

"Did you see that?" I asked the bellhop who was helping me with my bags. "He used air quotes on me."

"*No hablo inglés,*" he replied.

"Good."

Once I got to my room, I was able to put the arrival incident behind me. I couldn't be upset; I had my own infinity pool! Our room was facing the ocean, we had a huge shower and Jacuzzi tub, and there were two Coronas and some chips and salsa sitting out by the infinity pool with a little welcome note from the hotel. I drank both Coronas and thought about how romantic this place would be for a couple.

"That's a depressing thought to have, dummy," I said out loud to myself. Then I thought about how lucky I was that Jackie and I were such close friends that we could vacation together and not feel pressured to go down on each other.

*There you go, Sarah, that is a much funnier thought to have.*

It's impossible for me to relax when a bag is packed, so I unpacked my bag, leaving one entire side of drawers for Jackie, and counted the hangers in the closet to make sure that I left

an equal amount for her. I'm a very polite/anal vacation partner. Then I changed into my bikini and headed down to scope
out the lounge-chair situation so when Jackie arrived the next
day I'd be armed with the knowledge of what time we needed
to get to the pool if we wanted umbrellas. It's called being a
fucking professional.

On my walk to the pool, I saw a pelican on the beach with
a wave cresting in the background, so I snapped a picture. I
admired my photography skills, then texted the picture to
Jackie and wrote: "So pretty here!"

"Seriously? You send me a picture of a dirty fucking bird? I
wanna see the infinity pool!" she responded.

"I thought it was pretty!" I wrote back. "And since I'm in
Mexico that text cost me fifty cents so maybe be a little nicer."

"I'll give you fifty cents when I get there."

Jackie is also a polite vacation partner. I ran back up to the
room, took a picture of the infinity pool, texted it to her, and
then went downstairs for a poolside cocktail.

The pool at the hotel was everything I had dreamed it
would be: plenty of comfy chairs, a handful of waiters, and
very few other people. It's not that I need complete solitude
while sunbathing—if I did, I'd have relaxed by our private
infinity pool and ordered room service. But lots of people just
hold up the drink service, plus nobody is fooling me when
they sit in the pool for hours drinking without ever getting out
to pee. I know what you're doing in there and I don't like it.

I spoke to one of the waiters and got the lowdown on what

time Jackie and I should arrive the next day to ensure we had the best seats in the house, then ordered myself a margarita, grabbed a chair, and caught up on the latest *Us Weekly*. I was only there for a few minutes before someone came by to check on me. *Nice service,* I thought.

"You need to order drink for you husband?" the waiter asked.

"It's just me today," I sighed.

"Jus you?"

"Yeah, jus me!" I smiled and held the magazine up as close to my face as possible.

"Oh-kay," he replied.

*Did he just say "okay" with a super-sad tone in his voice?* I shrugged it off, ordered another margarita, and headed back to my room. The sun was starting to go down so I figured I'd get that writing in before Jackie arrived and all hell broke loose.

I had three or four more margaritas while I wrote in the hotel room. I wrote while lying on the bed, I wrote on the balcony, I even started to write while sitting in the infinity pool until I realized what a shitty idea that was now that I was tipsy. A couple hours later, after I got a pretty decent amount of work done and noticed I was making more typos than usual, I decided it was time for a meal that wasn't liquid. I put on a cute sundress and headed down to the hotel restaurant. (Don't worry; I leave the resort at some point in this story. But half-drunk and alone didn't seem like the safest option—I *was* still in Mexico, you guys.)

I approached the hostess station and asked for a table for dinner.

"For how many?" she asked me politely.

"Just one!" I said, probably louder than I needed to.

"Follow me!"

*Finally! Someone isn't giving me the third degree about dining alone, and of course it's a woman! Men are so stupid.*

She sat me at a nice table with a lovely view of the ocean and said my waiter would be right over. I felt so relaxed; the ocean always makes me feel that way. And there was a really light breeze and a gorgeous sunset. *This is perfect.*

A busboy approached the table and looked at me.

"*Hola!*" I greeted him.

"*Hola! Tú hablas español?*"

"*Un poquito,*" I replied.

Then he rattled off something I couldn't keep up with and I interrupted him: "*Muy poquito,*" I said apologetically. But people in Cabo are very accommodating to travelers from the United States. Almost everyone there speaks English, at least at the resorts, so when I am there I can continue to be a lazy visiting American who pays for stuff in US dollars.

"*No problema,*" he laughed. "You have someone joining you?"

Jesus Christ.

"Nope, just me!" I said for the one hundredth time.

"Jus you?"

"Jus me!" *What is this, fucking Groundhog Day?*

The busboy looked at me with what I am positive was pity while he began to clear the other place setting at the table. And he was making a pretty big scene about it, clanging glasses and bread plates together like it was his job—which I guess technically it was, but still.

I took a deep breath and looked back out at the ocean. The waiter approached and asked me what I wanted to drink.

"Margarita, rocks, no salt," I replied.

"Okay. You have someone joining you?" he asked.

*What. The. Fuck.*

"No, I don't have anyone joining me," I snapped. I was losing my patience. "See how there is only one place setting here? The busboy took the other one away because I am dining alone. So . . . one margarita, quickly, *por favor.*"

The waiter nodded and walked away, looking slightly confused.

Another waiter then approached my table, holding a basket of bread.

"You need more plate for bread?" he asked.

"No, one is fine," I replied curtly.

"Nobody else es coming?"

"What?"

"No fren is coming?" he asked.

"What? Yes, a friend is coming. She's just not here yet. Can I please have that bread?" It was as if he was holding it hostage.

The waiter stared at me blankly.

"I have a friend coming tomorrow. She missed her plane today because she was in a terrible car accident. The other person died and everything. But she'll be here tomorrow, so if it makes you feel better, you can bring another plate then."

The waiter set the basket of bread down and hurried away without saying a word.

*That should take care of that.* I smiled to myself proudly.

Finally my margarita arrived, with yet another waiter carrying it.

*Jesus, how many fucking people work at this place?* I wondered.

"*Hola,*" the fortieth waiter said as he set my drink down. "You ready to order or you wan to wait for you fren?"

"Seriously?"

"So you wan to wait then for you fren?"

"*I don't have a 'fren' coming tonight,*" I yelled, my patience now totally gone. "I'm dining alone. My friend will be here tomorrow. I just want to eat."

"So . . . only *uno*?" he asked.

"*What?*" I yelled.

"Only . . . *uno*?"

"Yeah, only *uno*. FUCKING *UNO. UUUUUUUUU-NO. Uno, Uno, Uno, UNO!* FUCK!" I suddenly realized I was now standing.

"Oh-kay," he said, and ran away without taking my order.

A few seconds later the second waiter returned to take my order. Clearly the third waiter was too afraid to come back. I ordered a steak and made a point of looking at my phone and laughing often, just to make everyone else feel at ease that I did in fact have friends, that those friends were texting me, and that their texts were *hilarious*.

I finished my meal rather quickly, signed the bill, and darted back to my room with a full margarita in hand. Immediately putting on my bathing suit, I lit some candles, and hopped into the infinity pool.

Ah, peace. Peace and silence. Nobody was asking me why I was alone, but I was and it was glorious. *Uno.* The moon cast an amazing light over the ocean and relaxation finally started to creep back in. That is, until I thought about how I'd had like ten margaritas by now and could possibly drown. In a hotel room. Alone. *UNO.* I climbed out of the pool, toweled off, and got into bed. I wasn't going to go out like that. Plus, dying before Jackie got there would be totally rude.

I spent the next morning inhaling room-service pancakes and soaking up some sun at the beach awaiting Jackie's arrival. I was halfway through a strawberry margarita when she texted me that she was en route to the hotel. I went back up to order some chips and salsa and two Coronas, wanting Jackie to have the same arrival experience that I had. When I got to the room, I was pleasantly surprised to find the aforementioned items already waiting for us. Apparently this was a daily service. *Nice touch,* I thought. Then I said a silent thank-you that today they didn't just leave one Corona—that might have sent me over the edge.

"This place is amazing!" Jackie yelped. As soon as she'd arrived, we jumped into the infinity pool to drink our Coronas and talk about how awesome this resort was.

"I know! Sooooo, did you get grilled by your driver about why you were alone?" I laughed.

"No. Why?" she responded.

"Really? Ugh. My driver asked me like a zillion questions about why I was alone and then when I said you were coming in today he just assumed we were lesbians."

"You wish," Jackie laughed.

"Ew. No I don't. I don't have any interest in being a lesbian. Vaginas are so weird looking."

"Maybe yours is, but mine isn't!" Jackie replied.

"That's not true, everyone's is!"

"How do you know?"

"I've seen other ones on the Internet."

Jackie laughed. "You have to just stop people from asking too many questions. The driver asked me why I was alone and I said I was engaged and meeting friends for a girls' trip before I get married. He didn't ask me any more questions."

"But you haven't even set the wedding date yet! You lied."

"Yeah, but I also didn't flip out on a waiter last night. Sometimes a white lie keeps things running smoothly," she explained.

"This doesn't mean I have to walk around with a crown of dicks on my head all weekend, does it?"

"No, if anyone would have to, it would be me. I'm the bachelorette, dumbass."

"Okay, good."

We polished off our Coronas, then headed down to the pool. I immediately found the guy I'd talked to the day before and he escorted us to two nice lounge chairs with an umbrella.

"Margarita, rocks, no salt?" he asked me.

*"Sí, gracias!"*

"I'll have the same," Jackie interjected. "I see you've already made your presence known at the bar," she continued as he walked away.

"Always."

Jackie and I spent the day wandering back and forth between the pool and the ocean, margaritas in tow. The drunker we got, the funnier my story from the previous evening became until we were just drunkenly yelling, "Only *UNO*?" at each other while I posed for Instagram photos in my bikini.

"No, not that one. You have to take it at an angle from above; that's what makes you look skinniest," I scolded her as I went through the last batch of photos she had taken of me. "Go stand on that rock and take another one."

"Jesus, this is a lot of work. I didn't know you cared so much about how you look in a stupid photo," she said in an accusatory tone.

"I'm single, Jackie. It matters how I look in the photos that I post on Instagram. I have a few possible suitors following me."

As much as I love my friends who are in relationships, sometimes I feel like they forget what it's like out there. And now with social media? We're all screwed.

After settling on a good photo, I told Jackie to get in the water so I could take a bikini picture of her to send to her fiancé, Brandon. We basically had a full-on photo shoot by the sea.

"Oh, that one is okay but I look really pale," Jackie noted as she scrolled through her options. "I can't send him that."

*Ah, people who are in relationships are human, too!* I thought happily.

"Don't worry, I'll put a nice filter on it—boom! You're tan!"

Jackie smiled proudly and told me to send the photo. "He's probably missing me right now, don't you think?"

"Definitely," I agreed as I texted it to him. "You almost look Brazilian in this. Damn, Instagram is *good*."

We went back to our room to get ready to go out. When I was getting dressed, I noticed a few bumps on my stomach. Then I turned around and realized they were on my back and on my legs, too. "Oh my God, bedbugs!" I yelled to Jackie.

She ran over and looked at my bump-ridden body. "Those aren't bedbug bites. I've had bedbugs, remember? I got them last time we were here."

I did remember. She'd gotten bedbugs when we were in Cabo for our friend Sarah Tilley's wedding. We were sharing a room and I didn't get them, which was weird but not something I was going to complain about.

"What else could they be? They're everywhere!" I yelled, on the verge of tears. I had planned on living in my bikini the next few days . . . this was not good.

"Maybe a heat rash? Or an allergic reaction? I'm not sure. Let's go down to the gift shop and see if they have some Cort-aid or something."

The woman working at the gift shop was stumped, but she also assured me they were not bedbug bites. "Believe me, I know bedbug bites. I'm Mexican."

"Well what else could it be?!" I asked.

"Maybe an allergy, yes. Or the heat. This should help clear it right up," she said as she handed me a Mexican version of Cortaid.

"Do you have the American version of Cortaid? Like . . . Cortaid?" I asked.

"Is fine, trus me. This will work," she laughed.

We went back to the room and I covered myself in the generic Mexican cream. I put on a dress that seemed to cover all the bumps so that people wouldn't think I was diseased, and then Jackie and I drank our complimentary Coronas (they just keep bringing them all day!) and headed out for a night on the town. I put on a brave face because I didn't want to ruin our first night of vacation, but inside my weird rash horrified me. I'm just not a fan of having weird shit on my body—but I guess nobody is.

Downtown Cabo is kind of what you'd expect: a bit of a mess with lots of techno clubs, a few good restaurants, plenty of bars, and a lot of drunk people. I noticed a lot of them looked like they were in college. Then when one group of super-intoxicated girls threw back a round of shots and yelled, "Spring break, wooooooo!" it dawned on me why.

"Oh my God, we are in Mexico during spring break," I told Jackie, kind of horrified.

"Well, the good news is, you probably aren't the only person in here who is going to develop a rash this weekend," she responded. Then she looked around, ordered us two shots of tequila, raised them up, and yelled, "Spring break, wooooooo!"

We spent the next couple of hours barhopping, yelling, "Spring break, woooooo!" It got funnier every time we did it, and we did it a lot. There were definitely tons of spring breakers around, but two guys our age zeroed in on us and offered us some seats at their table. One of them was really cute and the other one seemed to have a nice personality. If they had been girls, he would have been considered the "fat friend." He wasn't fat at all, but you know what I mean.

The cute one was flirting with Jackie, but she made it clear she was happily engaged. He seemed kind of disappointed but continued to train his attention on her. *Why am I stuck with the fat friend?* I thought. *Did the cute one notice the rash?*

We spent the rest of the night hanging out with cute guy and fat friend, the four of us getting pretty drunk. When the bar started to close Jackie suggested they come back to our hotel and drink. "We have an infinity pool, it's awesome!" she told them.

I grabbed Jackie by the arm and excused us to the bathroom. "You aren't doing anything bad, right?" I asked her when we were safely out of earshot.

"Fuck no! I just thought they were fun and maybe you can get some action. I'd never cheat on Brandon!"

"I know! I was just making sure because we're drunk. But I'm not getting any action; the cute one likes you and I'm not going to hook up with him just because he can't hook up with you. That's sad . . . for me."

"Well, what about the other guy?"

I realized then that neither of us had called them by name, because we had no idea what their names were.

"It's too late to ask," Jackie said. "So what about the other guy? You can hook up with him. He's totally into you."

"The fat friend?"

"He's not fat," Jackie laughed.

"I know, but he's technically the fat friend."

"Okay, fine, are you going to hook up with the fat friend?"

"I don't know," I said, pulling up my dress and looking in the bathroom mirror to see if my rash had spread. It had. "Oh my God, look! There are more bumps. That Mexican Cortaid made it worse!"

"Just give it time, it'll go away. Seriously, I think you should hook up with that guy, he's really nice."

"Lots of people are really nice; it doesn't mean I should hook up with them."

"You haven't had sex in almost a year," she reminded me.

"Good point. I'll hook up with him. No sex, but he can finger me. And I have to keep the lights off because of the rash."

"Done," Jackie agreed.

When the four of us got back to the hotel, Jackie immediately cracked open the minibar and started pouring drinks. I put my iPod on and started blaring country music. The cute one asked if I had any other music, which I did.

"Nope," I replied. "If you don't like country music you can leave." I said it with a tone that made him think I was being hilarious, but in reality I was being mad because he didn't like me. Then I put Luke Bryan on shuffle and turned the volume up as loud as I could.

"Is that going to piss off your neighbors?" Fat Friend asked.

"We don't have neighbors!" I yelled, excited about the fact that the room next to us was vacant.

"If we did they'd have to learn to love Luke Bryan," Jackie threw in. "It's not really an option not to when Sarah is around."

"True that," I said as I attempted to high-five her but stumbled and ended up slapping her in the face.

We both laughed hysterically and I began to croon "Buzz-kill" while Cute Guy and Fat Friend looked on in horror.

I kept drinking while periodically disappearing into the bathroom to check on the progression of my rash. It wasn't getting better, but it wasn't getting worse. I tried to let that stasis put my mind at ease.

Since we only had one room, letting Fat Friend finger me

was going to be tricky. I turned up "Country Girl" extra loud and pulled Jackie aside.

"Okay, how is this going to work?" I asked.

"Easy! Cute Guy and I will go in the infinity pool and I'll close the doors to the patio so Fat Friend can fiddle your vagina."

"You're going into the infinity pool with Cute Guy?" I asked, half-jealous.

"Yes, it's fine. All I've been doing is talking about Brandon, and I got him to talk about his ex-girlfriend so now he's just Sad Friend."

"Okay, perfect."

Jackie and Cute/Sad Guy splashed around in the infinity pool while Fat Friend awkwardly tried to dance with me to Luke Bryan's "Do I."

"We don't need to dance," I told him. I actually kind of wanted to, but he kept stepping on my feet and I had just gotten a pedicure.

He took my dance refusal as an invitation to do other things and went in for a kiss. It was a pretty decent kiss, so it turned into a full-on make-out session, with us tumbling onto the bed and me awkwardly trying to guide his hands around my rash.

"Am I doing something wrong?" he asked after the forty-seventh time I shoved his hand off of my stomach.

"No! Not at all!" I said, trying to reassure him. I was actually kind of enjoying the make-out session; it *had* been a long time since my last one and I didn't want to ruin it. "I'm sorry, I have a rash."

"Huh?" he responded, as expected.

"I don't know. I went to the beach today and I came back with a rash. I don't know what it is and it's really gross and I'm sorry—if you want to leave it's totally fine."

"A rash? It's Mexico. Of course you got a rash. Can I see it?"

"No!" I yelled, and slapped his hand away.

"Just let me see it. I'm not going anywhere." Fat Friend slowly pulled up my dress as I covered my eyes in shame.

"Those are bites. Maybe sand fleas, or what my mom used to call 'no-see-'ems,' because . . . because, you know, you can't see 'em."

"How do you know?"

"I've had them. I come here all the time. Trust me, they're no big deal."

"Well, Jackie didn't get them and we were at the same place all day."

"Her skin probably doesn't smell as sweet as yours . . ."

Fat Friend had *game*. I quickly forgot about my "no-see-'em" bites and let Fat Friend finger me as planned. I didn't even touch his penis, so it was a perfect night . . . for me.


The next morning, Jackie and I ordered an uncomfortable amount of room service and immediately began drinking again. Cute Guy and Fat Friend were long since headed to the airport to go home, wherever that was—in addition to never having learned their names, we also never learned where they lived *or* what they did for a living.

"Pool time?" Jackie asked as she poured us both a Bloody Mary.

"Yes!"

I changed into my bikini, noting that the bumps had not gotten any better.

"Fuck!" I complained.

"They haven't gotten any worse either," Jackie said encouragingly. "Glass half full!"

"My glass actually is half-full. Can you fill it before we head down to the pool?"

We spent the next couple of days doing exactly what we'd planned to do: drinking, tanning, reading, drinking, and posting pictures on Instagram to make our friends jealous. Something also attacked Jackie, but it appeared to be mosquitoes and they were only interested in her hands. So in every photo we had to make sure nobody could see my rash or her swollen knuckles. We were a real mess.

Time flew by and before we knew it, we were having our last night of dinner at The Office, a local restaurant with pretty good food and really great people-watching. A guy in a sombrero approached our table, shot glasses in hand and a whistle around his neck.

"We're good, we're in our thirties," I told him.

"Ignore her," Jackie interrupted. "Spring break, woooo!"

I giggled and we both did like four tequila shots, the waiter blowing a whistle and clapping after each one.

"Oh, Fat Friend just texted me," I called out to Jackie as I checked my phone. "I didn't even realize I gave him my phone number."

"What did he say?"

"That he had a great time and to stay in touch."

"Are you going to stay in touch?"

"No."

"Why not? You guys seemed to get along," she countered.

"We got along fine, sure. But that was mostly because I wanted to get fingered and he had a finger."

"Well, why not just see him again?"

"He was really nice, and it was a fun night, but it's not like there were real sparks or anything. Plus, he lives far away."

"Where?"

"I have no idea."

Jackie laughed. "Have you ever thought that maybe you stop relationships before they can start?"

"Are you trying to ruin my buzz?"

"I'm serious! You say you want to date someone, but then when you meet—"

"*You're a buzzkill every time you come around, those beers might as well have been poured out . . .*" I drunkenly sang my favorite Luke Bryan—who else?—song to her.

"Okay, fine. We don't have to talk about it . . . tonight.

By the way, I really like that song and I think Brandon might break up with me over it."

"Fat Friend didn't know the words, and that's how I know we aren't meant to be."


**A**s we packed for the airport the next day, we decided to go have one last morning margarita before heading out. We got our favorite seats by the pool and the waiter brought us drinks that we didn't even have to order.

"I love this place," I told Jackie as I dipped my toes in the pool.

"Me too," she agreed.

"Thanks for coming with me. I know you have a boyfriend who you could go on vaca—"

"Shut up," Jackie interrupted. "I had a blast and just because I have a boyfriend doesn't mean I don't want to spend time away with you."

"I know; I just hope you didn't come because you feel sorry for me. Like you know I don't have a guy to go with so you told Brandon you had to come with me so I don't kill myself or something."

Jackie laughed. "I already told you, you could 'have a guy' if you want one. You're just not looking. I know you say you are, but you're not. I'm also not worried about it. You're going to be fine; you always are. You put a lot of work into having the career you've always wanted, and when you're ready you'll put the same amount of work into your personal life. Plus I think being single for a while is a good thing."

"Wow. You really think that?"

"I really think that."

"Thanks, Jackie. That means a lot. I actually think being single is really good right now, too. I just sometimes wonder if I like being single too much . . ." I started to tear up.

"There's no crying in Cabo," Jackie said.

I laughed. "True. But there is fingering!"

"Spring break, woooo!" Jackie chimed in.

As we got ready to leave, I got a text alert that my flight was delayed two hours. Jackie was on a different flight and hers was on time.

"Go ahead, I'm gonna stay here for a little bit longer," I told her. "I don't want to sit at that terrible airport that long by myself."

Jackie and I hugged and had a stranger take one more Instagram photo of us, and then she took off.

I decided I was hungry, so I walked up to the restaurant to grab some lunch while I awaited further notice on my flight.

"How many?" the waiter asked me as he looked behind me, expecting to see someone else.

"*Uno,*" I replied.

"Only *uno?*"

"Yes, only *uno,*" I said proudly, and he walked me to my table without saying another word.

## What Ails Me?

I find that the older I get, the more time I spend on WebMD researching a variety of possible ailments, real or imagined, and diagnosing myself. Recently, I convinced myself that I was suffering from early-onset menopause. I was just shy of turning thirty-nine at the time, so I knew that it would be *super*-early-onset menopause, but I found myself sweating profusely at night, and the only possible explanation for waking up in a pool of sweat that made sense based on my Internet search was "the change of life." I sat in my gynecologist's office and explained to my doctor, whom I have been going to for about fifteen years, that even though I was only thirty-eight years and three hundred forty-seven days old, I was experiencing the inevitable end of my menstrual cycle and thus, my youth.

"Well, if that's the case, you're experiencing it very, very early . . . but it can happen."

"I knew it," I said, satisfied with my keen self-diagnosis.

"I didn't say it was happening to you, I just said it can happen. But it isn't that common. What exactly are your symptoms?"

"I wake up in pools of sweat. Like I-need-to-change-the-sheets-the-next-day kind of sweat. I mean, I don't actually change them but I should."

"Okay, what else?" she asked.

"That's it."

"That's it?"

"Isn't that enough? Who sweats when they sleep? It's not like it's hard work."

"Well, have you tried turning on your air conditioner?" she said jokingly.

"Ha ha, very funny. Seriously, it's obviously menopause. Can you give me something to slow it down? Or maybe even speed it up? I don't really *need* to have my period, it just gets in the way."

"I really don't think you're experiencing menopause. But it might be something hormonal . . ."

"Yeah, something hormonal would be menopause!" I told her as if I was the one with the medical degree.

"All right," she said, trying to politely get more information out of me, "we can do some hormone testing."

"Great. Oh! And I'm also coughing a lot at night. Like I wake myself up coughing this dry, awful cough."

"Huh. Really? Are you also coughing during the day?" she

asked in what sounded like the tone of someone who's taking notes, yet she wasn't holding a clipboard or even a pen.

"A little, but it's worse at night."

"Sarah, I think you have the flu."

"Is that also a sign of early menopause?"

"No, it's a sign of the flu."

"I don't think that's what I have."

"Are you also a little more tired than usual?" she asked, still seemingly making check marks on her mental notepad.

"Well, yes, but that's because I'm not getting a lot of sleep since I keep waking up sweating and coughing because of the *me-no-pause*," I explained slowly.

"*Or* it's because you have the flu. There's a nasty strain going around right now. I'll prescribe you something that will help ease the symptoms, and if that plus a couple days of rest doesn't take care of it, you can come back and tell me more about your menopause."

"I guess we can give that a try for now, but I'll probably be back soon for those tests," I replied, eyeing her skeptically.

"Can't wait." She smiled and handed me a prescription.

About five days later, I received a call from her office, checking in to see how I was feeling.

"I'm okay," I said to the receptionist, not wanting to fully admit that my menopause symptoms had completely cleared up since they had been treated with a flu remedy and some rest. "For now, anyway . . ."

"Okay, I will let the doctor know your flu is gone," he said.

"That's not what I—"

"See you for your next annual checkup, Sarah!" he said cheerily, and hung up.

Ugh, the whole office was so smug with the whole "flu" diagnosis. I sort of wished there was a way to catch menopause just so I could go back and tell her that her medical degree was no match for my superior Internet research skills.

If you think I learned to stop self-diagnosing after this incident, you are mistaken.

A couple of months later, I was feeling like I was being extra bitchy to people, so I decided to go to the doctor to find out what was behind it. I opted not to go to my gynecologist this time, fearing she might say something practical, like "Just stop being so bitchy," so I asked around and located a doctor who specialized in hormone testing. I figured this way, when someone accused me of being a bitch, I could blame it on a condition that was out of my hands, and in turn make them feel bad for picking on me while I was sick and possibly dying.

The doctor's office was located in Beverly Hills on the tenth floor of a ten-floor building, so I assumed this doctor was no shit. I mean, that's like the equivalent of living in the penthouse, you know? However, when I arrived I was slightly disappointed to see that it was a tiny office and there were boxes piled up everywhere, leaving little room for seating.

"Are you guys moving?" I asked the receptionist.

"No," she said flatly, not acknowledging the large box overflowing with papers on top of her desk. "Just bring this back to me when you're finished filling it out," she continued as she handed me a clipboard full of forms.

I sat down on one of the two sad plastic chairs in the "waiting room" and propped my feet up on a box while I filled out the standard intake forms. I usually fly right through the columns, knowing the answer to all of them is "no," because I don't have any heart conditions (that I know of), I don't have diabetes (that I know of), I'm not pregnant (that I know of), and I've never had surgery of any kind . . . wait, have I?

"Excuse me," I called out to the receptionist, who was wrapping something ceramic in newspaper.

"Yes?" she asked, annoyed.

"Is Botox considered surgery?"

"No," she said, rolling her eyes.

"I mean, it's not like I've had a lot," I told her, feeling the need to defend myself. "I just get a little between the eyebrows. It was starting to look like I had a number eleven on my forehead."

"Uh-huh." She was disinterested.

"I'd show you what I mean, but I can't make the number eleven there anymore because of the Botox. That stuff really works, you know."

"Uh-huh," she repeated as she put the item wrapped in newspaper into a box.

"You sure you guys aren't moving?" I asked, pressing her.

"We're not moving. Are you done with your forms? The doctor will see you now."

"Wow, that was quick," I said as I handed her the clipboard. "Usually doctors take forever. This is great!"

*But is it great?* I wondered. *Why isn't he a little busier? At least make me wait twenty minutes for show or something.*

Mrs. Personality led me into a room, took my blood pressure, and weighed me.

"One hundred thirty-five pounds," she said in what felt like the loudest voice in the world.

"One hundred thirty-five?!" I repeated in a panicked whisper. "That can't be right. I weigh one hundred and twenty-eight pounds. Weigh me again, I'll take my shoes off."

She looked down at my blue Havaianas, then back up at me. "You think your flip-flops weigh seven pounds?"

I really didn't like this bitch. "Forget it. Obviously your scale is off. Or maybe it's because of whatever is wrong with my hormones."

"What's wrong with your hormones?" she asked, genuinely interested now.

"I don't know, that's why I'm here. Can I see the doctor now, please?"

"He'll be right in. He's just finishing up some packing."

"Packing? So you *are* moving!"

"No, we're not moving," she said as she exited the room.

*What the fuck is going on in this place?*

A couple minutes later, the doctor came in, planted himself in a little chair on wheels, and rolled over to the exam table, where I was sitting.

"Good afternoon, Ms. Corona."

"It's Colonna."

"Ah. Good afternoon, Ms. Corona."

"No, Co*lo*nna," I repeated.

He just sat there blinking at me. WTF?

"Good afternoon," I said, giving up.

"So what brings you here today?"

Ugh. I hate when they ask you that after you've just spent fifteen minutes filling out forms explaining what brought you there today—the same forms they appear to be studying while you repeat exactly what's written down.

"I haven't been myself lately; I think there's something wrong with my hormones."

"What do you mean by 'haven't been yourself'?" he asked, taking notes. Seeing him take notes actually made me uneasy. My gynecologist didn't need to take notes; why did he?

"Well, I've been very . . . on edge."

"What do you mean by 'on edge'?" he repeated in the exact same voice in which he'd asked the last question.

"What do I mean by 'on edge'?" I repeated sarcastically. "I mean that I am on edge . . . like more than usual."

"Uh-huh, I can see that," he said as he jotted something down.

"No, I'm not on edge right now, I just mean in general lately I've been a little more on edge."

"You seem a little on edge right now, Ms. Corona," he said with a weird lilt in his voice like he was kind of enjoying irritating me.

"Well, I wasn't on edge when I walked in here, but yeah, you're right: I'm a little on edge now."

"And why do you think that is?" he asked as he pushed his glasses up the bridge of his large nose.

*Is this guy fucking serious?*

"Dr. Goldstein—"

"Gold*berg*."

"I'm sorry—Dr. Goldstein. I'm not really here to talk about my feelings; I mean, you aren't a therapist."

"Do you see a therapist regularly?" he asked as he jotted down yet another note.

This guy was really getting on my nerves. Yes, I was feeling extra bitchy. But this doctor was prodding me and I couldn't figure out why. Everything he said was in a tone I couldn't quite put my finger on but I knew I didn't like it.

"Doctor," I said in a very calm voice, "I'm not here to discuss my mental health with you. I feel like you want me to but I don't want to do that. I'm just here to find out why I've been super bitchy lately and also how it's possible that I gained seven pounds since I left the house this morning."

"*Oh!* You've noticed weight gain?!" he shouted almost gleefully.

"Well, I noticed it when your receptionist weighed me, yeah."

"Well, that is my specialty," he said proudly.

I looked around the office and noticed several different posters for several different kinds of weight-loss supplements.

"Wait, is this a weight-loss clinic?" I asked, confused.

"No, no, no. Not at all," he laughed (which was weird). "I see patients for all kinds of reasons, usually hormone-related treatments, which I assume is how you found me, right?"

"Well, yeah, I think so," I said, trying to remember how I did find him. Was it Yelp? TripAdvisor? Craigslist?

"I specialize in hormone imbalances. It's just that many times, especially in females, hormone imbalances lead to weight gain, and I have a very high success rate in helping women lose that extra weight."

Well, that wasn't what I had come in for, but I figured if I left the office with a few diet pills it wouldn't be the worst outcome.

"But let's focus on why you're here, okay?"

"Okay," I said, relaxing a little.

"So why are you here?"

*I'm going to kill myself.*

"The thing I said about being bitchy, remember? The conversation we had like four minutes ago?" I said, my voice rising in annoyance.

"Okay, okay, yes. That. All right, I'm going to do some general hormone testing and we will go from there. It's possible you have too much testosterone in your system, which can sometimes lead to 'edginess' and even weight gain."

"Well, obviously I have too much testosterone in my body, Doctor. Listen to my voice. And this afternoon I watched an entire hockey game . . . on TV. I definitely have too much testosterone. How about you check my estrogen and see if it's . . . there?"

"Oh, I love hockey. Which is your team?"

"I don't have one! That's why it's weird that I watched an entire hockey game on TV. Seriously. I think I need estrogen."

"Okay, we will get to the bottom of this. The nurse will come in and take some blood samples, then we'll call you when the results are in, you'll come back to see me, and we'll go over them. Sound good?"

"Sure. Will you guys be here or at your new location then?" I asked, hoping to trick him into admitting they were moving. I'm nothing if not persistent.

"What new location?"

"Well, there are boxes everywhere. And the receptionist was wrapping stuff up. And she said you were packing . . ."

"Oh, no, I was packing for a weekend trip, that's all."

"Oh. Well, what is she packing for?"

"She's just keeping busy," he said as he smiled and walked out the door.

The nurse came in right after, took my blood samples, and told me I could go home. When I walked out, there was still nobody else in the waiting room. I looked over at the receptionist, who was now taking things *out* of boxes and putting them away. Clearly, business was slow. That couldn't be a great sign for either of us.

--- --- ---

**A** week later, the receptionist took a break from wrapping knickknacks for no reason to call me and tell me my results were ready. Of course, she wouldn't give them to me over the phone; I had to go in and see Dr. Annoying again.

"Good to see you again, Ms. Cabana," Dr. Goldberg said as he sat on his little rolly stool and scooted over to greet me.

"Hello, Dr. Silverstein. So you have my results?"

"Yes."

"Great. What do you got for me?"

"Well, your hormone levels are pretty normal for the most part. But I did find one thing that I need to inform you about."

I took a deep breath and readied myself to hear about how I had a hormone imbalance that was making me edgy, but worse . . . also giving me cancer.

"Your FSH levels are very low."

"Whoa," I said as I took another deep breath. "What's an FSH level?"

"Well, that's your fertility hormone. It means that you have a very low chance of being able to get pregnant."

"Oh!" I said, relieved. "Okay. So when those levels are low do women tend to get more mood swings?"

"Not that I'm aware of, it simply indicates that if you want to get pregnant, you probably cannot."

"Well, that's okay because I don't want to get pregnant. What else did you find? There must be a reason why I'm so mean to people, particularly ones who are in front of me in line at the Coffee Bean."

"I don't think you understand. You have about a two percent chance of getting pregnant."

"Is there a way to make it zero percent?" I asked, not at all joking.

"This is something you need to understand. If you decide you want children—"

"I don't want children."

"But if you change your mind—"

"I'm not going to change my mind."

"Women say that but then they often change their minds, and I'm telling you that you would be unable to—"

"Doctor? I get it. It's fine."

"But, Ms. Carson—"

"It's Colonna. My last name is *Colonna*. I've told you that no less than eighty times."

"I'm sorry, Ms. *Colonna*," he repeated slowly and carefully. "This news appears to have upset you. Would you like some time alone to process the fact that your body may not ever be able to give you a child?"

"The news hasn't upset me, *you've* upset me."

"Excuse me?" he asked.

"I told you I understand. And you keep trying to tell me you know better than I do how I feel about children. Here's the thing: I just don't want kids. It doesn't make me weird, it doesn't mean that I don't like kids or that I want to punch them. Although I did recently see a baby who had his own seat in first class and I did want to punch him a little on my way to my economy seat right next to the lavatory."

"You seem on edge."

"Am I on a hidden-camera show? The edginess is the reason I'm here in the first place. I don't need you to tell me anything except what's on that piece of paper. I am not trying to get pregnant, ever. I've spent most of my adult life trying *not* to get pregnant. In fact, sometimes after sex, I turn on my blow-dryer and hold it right up to my vagina because when I was in high school, Kristy Stewart told me that can keep you from getting pregnant. I'm thirty-eight years old and that's still my move. Understand?"

"Not really," he said.

"I know you don't. And I don't expect you to. But let me just give you a piece of advice: if you're going to try to make a woman feel bad about the status of her ovaries, at least have the decency to get her fucking name right."

With that, I stormed out of the office, past the still-packing receptionist, and out the front door.

Three seconds later, I walked right back in to find the doctor still sitting in the exam room, looking bewildered.

"Can I still get some of those diet pills?"

"I'm sorry, but you're not overweight enough for diet pills," he replied.

I stared at him for a minute, then smiled. "That's more like it, Doctor. That's how you talk to a woman."

## Called Up to the Majors

Due to my love for baseball, I've always dreamed of becoming a baseball wife. Now that I'm in my thirties and a little smarter, I realize that may not turn out so great for me . . . or for anyone who wants a husband who doesn't bang a bunch of other women when he's on the road. Yes, I know there are a few good ones who don't do that—I'm generalizing here—but based on my past choices, I'm being realistic about which type I'd be drawn to; unfortunately, I doubt it would be one of the "good ones."

So aside from funny people and friends, I follow a handful of baseball players on Twitter. Social media has opened a whole new world in communication with complete strangers. It's not something that my friends and I had to deal with when we were in high school and college, thank God. But now, social media is prevalent in everyone's life, young and old. Facebook is where everyone goes to spy on and judge people we haven't seen in years, or scope out photos on a new love interest's page to determine if there is any stiff competition lingering around. There are apps like Tinder where people go to "meet other people," which really means "fuck other people," because what kind of relationship is really going to start with a swipe to the right? And Twitter is just a whole big combination of it all, with the added bonus that for networking, it's a sea of opportunity.

I interact with Twitter followers more than anyone I know, perhaps to a fault. When I dare take a vacation, or, God forbid, go out to dinner and refuse to look at my phone, some followers yell at me for "ignoring" them. I even respond to those people later, defending my right to stay off my phone for hours at a time, which is totally counterproductive. But I've built my Twitter bed, so I have to tweet in it.

The communication goes further than that, though. People who don't know each other follow each other and start sending direct messages back and forth. I've become friendly with funny women like Kelly Oxford and Jenny Johnson this way. But it's a "club" of sorts. We know each other's work, but we've never met, so we just direct-message (DM) and *boom*, now we are social-media buddies. It's all very intimate.

Single men follow hot women in hopes of this same result. Single women follow hot men for that reason, too. Of course, sometimes married men and women follow other attractive men or women, because said people are "funny" or "informative," but really they're hoping for a weird Internet affair. It happens.

Combining my love of baseball and my appreciation for social media, one day I decided to send a nice little tweet to one of the baseball players I follow, letting him know that he was one of my favorites. I didn't really think he'd respond, but I figured it never sucks to hear someone thinks you're awesome, right? A little later he sent me a direct message saying, "Thank you! I like your work!" Please keep in mind that you can only direct-message people when you follow each other, which meant he was now following me on Twitter. This was back in the earlier days of Twitter when pretty much nobody else was following me. You guys, this was exciting! Also, I need a life.

I got pretty worked up that Baseball Player had messaged me, and by "worked up," I mean "horny." The timing of the tweet couldn't have been better; it was the night before opening day of baseball season. I was at a bar at the time (shocking, I know) and immediately showed the message to my friend Chris. He got equally excited for me, as he'd also like to see me with a boyfriend in the MLB (he figures through me he could get hooked up with decent seats), so we carefully constructed my response. It was something along the lines of: "Thank you so much!!! Happy opening day tomorrow!" Sadly, it took us like two hours to construct it; we weren't all that sober.

The next day, I was on my way down to the Angels game with two of my girlfriends, Tara and Stephanie. They were also very, very worked up about my newfound friendship with Baseball Player, and by "worked up," I still mean "horny."

We were en route when I got a response from Baseball Player. I read it to the girls: "It says 'Thank You' and there's a smiley face."

The smiley face threw me off at first since he's a man *and* a professional athlete, but I've since reconciled with the fact that everyone loves emoticons, even grown men . . . in fact, now I do, too. I can't even bring myself to think about what life would be like without emoticons.

"A *smiley face*? But he's a professional baseball player!" Tara noted.

"Maybe he's an emotional one," I said, defending him.

"Smiley face or not, you need to give him your phone number," Stephanie demanded.

"I agree, but you can't just send your phone number out to the world!" Tara chimed in.

"She won't send it to the world, Tara, she can DM it to him. He *follows* her!"

"What's a DM?" Tara asked.

Stephanie rolled her eyes. Poor Tara, she is such a normal, non-social-media-obsessed person.

"It means I can send him a private message and nobody else will see it," I explained.

"That's amazing. What's a private message?" Tara asked.

"We don't have time to walk through all the mechanics of this for you, Tara, let's just get him Sarah's phone number, okay?"

Tara agreed, then we all debated how to send him the message. I was nervous, though. Why was I sending him my phone number? We hadn't even met! "What if he's just trying to be nice, or just be friends, and all of a sudden I send my number all aggressive-like and creep him out?"

"He's a *Major League Baseball player*," Stephanie retorted. "*That's* your reason for sending him your phone number if you think you need a reason, but I don't think he gives a shit about your motivation."

Moments later I sent Baseball Player a DM, saying that we should get a drink next time his team was in town playing. And of course, I included my phone number to "make it easier to get in touch with me."

Tara, Stephanie, and I continued to enjoy our vodka sodas aboard the Amtrak, my favorite transportation method to Angel Stadium (a.k.a. "the Big A"). Seconds later, I received a text message: "Hey there, it's me, plug my number in!"

My vagina exploded. Tara and Stephanie's vaginas exploded a little as well; they really wanted me to get penetrated by Baseball Player . . . they're good friends.

Next came a series of texts that were mostly constructed by Tara and Stephanie, as I was too nervous/excited/dumb to have any idea how to respond on my own.

"Tell him to have a great game today," Stephanie ordered.

"Tell him you're wearing a low-cut shirt," Tara suggested.

"Ask him where he stays when the team comes to town," Stephanie chimed in.

"Tell him you're not wearing any underwear!" Tara demanded.

"Okay, too far," Steph said.

"I agree. Plus, I am wearing underwear; I don't want our relationship to start out with a lie."

A compromise was made and I ended up texting him a photo of the three of us, now in our seats at the Big A, beers in hand, carefully featuring my deep V-neck T-shirt and zero reference to whether or not I was wearing underwear.

"You need one of my shirts," Baseball Player responded.

Was that a statement or a flirt? I couldn't tell. "What is he talking about? Why do I need one of his shirts? Does he mean mine is too low-cut and I look like a slut and he wants me to cover myself up like a lady?"

"He's a *Major League Baseball player*," Stephanie retorted. "He means you should be wearing one of his shirts, like from *his* team . . . duh!"

"Exactly . . . and he wants it on the floor of his bedroom," Tara explained.

"We'll handle this," Stephanie said as she grabbed my phone.

I was terrified, but I allowed the girls to take complete charge of the situation. I clearly didn't know what I was doing.

"Send me one of your shirts, then when you're in town you can help me take it off . . . ," Stephanie typed *from my phone*.

I was horrified. "This is too much too soon!" I told her. "He's going to think I'm coming on too strong. He's going to think I'm a *slut*!"

"He's a *Major League Baseball player*," Stephanie explained. "He loves sluts."

"You don't know a thing about him," I argued. "Maybe he wants a nice girl who doesn't send slutty things about getting naked with him the first time she meets him!"

"Then he doesn't want you, anyway, so what do you have to lose?" Tara asked.

*Solid point.*

We all held hands and waited for his response. Silence. No response. He had been texting me back immediately thus far and now, nothing.

"I knew it. He just wants to be friends, or maybe he thought I was a decent girl, and now he thinks I'm slutty. I can't believe I let you guys write that! This is so humiliating."

"He's a *Major League Baseball player*," Stephanie reiterated. "He doesn't want to be your friend; he already has friends . . . other *Major League Baseball players*."

"Maybe he's a nice guy," I said, trying to defend him again. "And now you've gone and ruined it."

I tried to shake off my disappointment and enjoy the game in front of me . . . the beer helped.

A couple of hours later, my phone vibrated. A text message.

The girls stared at me. "Is it *him*? What did he say?" they asked.

"I can't look," I whined.

"I can," Tara yelled as she grabbed my phone. She and Steph looked at the message and smiled.

"Well, what did he say?" I asked, sweating.

"Oh, this is good!" Steph exclaimed.

"Soooo good!" Tara added.

"Well, what the fuck did he say?" They were killing me.

"'Ooooh, that sounds fun. Too bad I'm not in town right now' . . . along with that smiley-face emoticon with the tongue hanging out," Steph read. "He really likes those emoticons."

"He's obviously sensitive! But what took him so long to write that? Do you think he had to ask his friends how he should respond?" I wondered.

"Sure, that must be it, he didn't know how to respond to a girl flirting with him, it's never happened to him before . . . that or it's *fucking opening day* and he has a game in an hour and he was warming up or taking batting practice," Tara explained rationally, but in a way that let me know I was really stupid.

*God, she's smart (except about Twitter).*

The rest of the day we enjoyed the game and intermittently discussed my future as the girlfriend of Baseball Player.

Later that night, I was home—now sans Tara and Stephanie—when my text alert went off.

"How was the game?" Baseball Player asked.

*Oh, shit. How was the game? I don't know! I don't have my friends here to tell me how it was!*

I texted them so they could help me tell Baseball Player how the game was, but they were both asleep like normal people. I was on my own, and I was drunk.

*Come on, Sarah, you can do this. You're an adult; you can*

*send a text message without having your friends tell you what to write.*

I took a deep breath. "It was great." No, that's stupid. It *was* great, but that's not the kind of response Tara and Steph would instruct me to give. I channeled their advice and started over.

"It was really fun, but would've been more fun if you'd been there to escort me home." I stared at the text for two whole minutes then took a deep breath and hit "send."

(Not bad, right?! *And* I'd thought of it all on my own!)

"That could've ended up being pretty fun," Baseball Player quickly wrote back.

"Well, hopefully soon you'll find out just how much fun I can be," I wrote back, without even thinking about it. Man, I was getting good. Tara and Steph *who*?

"It's a plan," he responded.

I immediately Googled his team's calendar. He was going to be in town in less than two months. I decided I'd go on a diet right away, then thought about it some more and figured I'd just wait until three days before he was in town and drink only juice for those three days; a much more realistic goal for me.

For the next few weeks, Baseball Player and I exchanged text messages. Flirts, photos (nothing too dirty; I never want my boobies on the Internet because my parents, although not completely savvy, do know how to use it), but mostly, we talked about getting together next time he was in town. That day was approaching and I couldn't wait; the buildup was killing me.

So, imagine my disappointment when I realized that when he was *in* town, I was going to be *out* of town doing stand-up for my book tour. *Fuck. My. Life.*

I'd been working so hard on this tour, been out of town so much, that the only personal life I had at this point was my text relationship with Baseball Player (probably not great, considering there was a pretty good chance *I* was not *his* only "personal life"). And now this book tour was going to keep me from getting out of the texting zone and into the penetration zone.

"This fucking book tour is ruining everything," I texted him.

"No, it's so great and so good for you!" he responded. "We play there two more times this year; we'll see each other then."

*Oh, God. He's so supportive of my career, like a good boyfriend should be.*

As we both continued our various travels, we kept in touch. One afternoon when he was in Seattle, he sent me a picture of the gloomy gray sky that said, "I don't know how people live here . . . it's so depressing."

*Ahhhh, he's feeling down.*

What makes people feel better when they're down? *Flowers!* And he's missing the sun . . . *sunflowers!* I immediately went online to have some sunflowers sent to his hotel but then stopped. I knew I wasn't allowed to make this decision on my own. Also, I didn't know what hotel he was staying in—there are a few in Seattle.

Tara and Stephanie liked the flowers idea; they thought it was sweet.

"Why not? I doubt he's been sent flowers very often," Tara said. "He'll think it's cute!"

Steph said to just text him and ask where he's staying. "Just ask him what hotel they stay in, because you go to Seattle a lot and are wondering if it's one of your faves."

"But I don't go to Seattle a lot."

Silence on the other end of the phone.

"Oh," I said. "Okay, I get it. Just *pretend . . .*"

Tara sighed and they both got off the phone so I could order the flowers. And *yes*, we do three-way phone calls as if we're still in high school.

I was nervous, so I consulted one more person: my friend Liz. She has been divorced once and engaged another time, but that time they broke up before they got married. She tells me I should always ask her advice about guys, because she's had two rings and I've had zero. In fact, she calls herself "Two Rings" when giving me advice and insists she knows better. I never retort that she no longer has either of those rings, so maybe her advice isn't the best to take, because when I'm feeling uncertain her logic makes sense.

Two Rings liked the idea of the sunflowers. She said it was "thoughtful" and that in his profession he probably didn't meet a lot of thoughtful women, "just a bunch of whores."

*Thanks, Two Rings.*

I decided the idea of getting myself into a more esteemed category than "whore" sounded nice, so I logged on to

1800Flowers.com to send some sunshine to Baseball Player, along with a note that said, "Since the sun isn't there, I'm sending you a little . . ."

*I'M SO SWEET! I can't believe I'm single!*

I nervously anticipated his response—this felt like a pretty bold move. A few hours later, he sent me a text with a photo of the flowers attached and wrote: "You're so sweet!" (*Told you!*)

I smiled and clicked on the image of the flowers to admire my work and was horrified to find that 1800Flowers.com did not send Baseball Player the sunflowers I had requested. Instead, it was just an arrangement of various flowers with like one-and-a-half sunflowers shoved in the middle. So now my sweet idea *because of his text about no sun* made no sense and it just looked like I randomly sent him a bouquet that looked like something you'd only send to a baseball player if it was for his funeral.

I immediately wrote back: "That was supposed to be all sunflowers! To send you sun in Seattle. Ugh, nobody ever listens to me."

He wrote back "Haha," and that was it. I was mortified. He probably picked the flowers up at the front desk, after his game, with all of his teammates standing right behind him, asking him who had died. *Ugh, I'm such a loser. A sweet loser, but a loser nonetheless.*

I immediately called Tara and Steph and told them my life was ruined, then I called Two Rings and told her that next time

I wanted her to give me advice, I was going to remind myself that two *failed* rings doesn't necessarily trump my zero rings. She laughed; it's something I've said to her like thirty-seven times. Then she came over and brought me a bottle of vodka.

I felt like communication from Baseball Player tapered off a little after that. I might have just been paranoid, but it didn't seem like he was as flirty as he was before. And the texts were coming a little less frequently. God, I hated flowers.

To make things worse, daily, I'd get an e-mail from 1800Flowers.com reminding me that I'd sent a big dumb bouquet of flowers to a *Major League Baseball player*. For some reason, I couldn't seem to unsubscribe. I swear I tried—it was like a mean joke was being played on me every time I checked my e-mail.

Of course, I kept Tara and Steph updated on any and all conversation between Baseball Player and me. They figured he was just busy and soon things would "heat up" again.

They were right. Out of nowhere, our texting picked up again.

"Maybe he suffered a concussion and forgot about the flowers!" I happily told Tara and Steph.

They agreed, but also suggested enough was enough. This back-and-forth, high-and-low, was too much for them to take anymore. They informed me it was time to take this texting relationship to the next level: sex.

"He won't be here until the end of the summer," Tara said. "That's too far away."

Steph and I agreed and so together, over margaritas, we pored over his team's schedule and came up with a plan.

"A *game* plan!" I said proudly, and laughed.

Tara and Steph just looked at me.

"Maybe don't lead off with one of your 'jokes' when you meet him," Steph suggested gently.

"But . . ." I started to defend myself and my "jokes."

"Sweetie, no," Tara said flatly.

"Okay."

So the *game* plan (they aren't here to judge me right now) was this: he would be in San Francisco in a few short weeks and I would fly up for a game and some long-time-in-coming "doing it."

Unsure of how to proceed, the girls suggested I inform him of the possibility of my having the weekend free when he was only a short flight away and told me to ask him if he thought he'd have time to "take me out for a drink."

"Of course!" he quickly replied. "Do it, come see me."

The plan was in motion. I booked my flight.

"Look, he's a *Major League Baseball player*," Stephanie said (this had become her favorite thing to say). "He probably has a ton of twentysomething-year-old girls after him. You need to show him that you have your own career, your own money, and that he doesn't need to take care of you. You need to show him that you can travel the same way he is used to traveling. You can be his *equal*."

"Oh, you mean like how I needed to show him how thoughtful I am by sending him fucking flowers like a big dumb asshole?"

Steph and Tara stood behind their decision to tell me to send the flowers and disagreed that it had any kind of negative impact on our blossoming (pun intended) relationship.

"He probably doesn't even think about it," Tara chimed in. I wasn't sure if that was good or bad, but I hoped she was correct.

Eager to show off my ability to travel like a big girl, I booked a huge suite at the Four Seasons. Fuck it; I'd been working my ass off. At this point I'd been out of town almost every weekend and my personal life was still suffering. I couldn't meet men when I was on the road. I couldn't "hook up" with guys I met at my shows; I didn't want that kind of reputation. However, I could fly up to San Francisco and let a *Major League Baseball player* put it in me (by "it," I mean "his penis"). Plus, I was pretty sure the only people who would know about my slutty adventure would be the friends I told, and I wasn't telling many. I suppose this chapter kind of ruins that theory, but I'm trying to paint a picture for you guys of what this certain period of my life was like, *okay*?

Steph's statement about "a ton of twentysomething-year-old girls after him" stuck in my head. I needed to compete with more than just my pretty-decent income. I needed to pull out the big guns.

So I booked a series of body wraps.

The woman at the spa I made the appointments with was a little crazy, in a good way . . . whatever that means—I think it's some sort of compliment.

Body-Wrap Lady poured me tea, measured my body fat, and made me drink alkalizers. I didn't know what an alkalizer was; it sounded like something you'd use to measure your blood-alcohol content. Actually, I didn't know what any of the stuff she was having me ingest was or what it was supposed to do, but she seemed to think it would make me thinner, and she was the pro, so I drank it.

She wrapped me in towels that were soaked in some sort of detox concoction and talked to me about what I was "holding on to" in my body that made me feel bloated. She got very philosophical about things and during each appointment I shed water weight in both sweat and tears. The tears came when she would diagnose some sort of mental or emotional block in me that caused my body to "grab on to fat and never let go," but they probably had more to do with the fact that it was like one hundred and forty degrees underneath all the towels.

I ended up spilling my guts to her; I figured why hold back secrets with someone who had seen me completely naked, covered my body in a charcoal scrub, and wrapped every inch of me like a mummy?

After hearing all the details I could remember while suffering from heatstroke, Body-Wrap Lady told me I was being too assertive with Baseball Player. She said he couldn't feel like a man if I was flying myself around and putting myself up in a hotel.

*WAIT, WHAT?*

This was the opposite of what Tara and Steph told me. So I explained to her that I was showing him I could do my own thing, unlike the twentysomethings who were chasing him around. She shook her head and said, "A man still has to feel like a man."

She suggested I take photos of different parts of my body— like my leg and the "sexy" part of my arm (wherever that is)— then tell him there was "more to see" when I met him in the hotel.

This sounded kind of fun, and it didn't involve a picture of my boobs or my Tweaky (I started calling it that when I was six years old). So that night I put on a little black dress and a pair of heels and attempted to take a sexy shot of my leg. But with every photo, I found a weird freckle or angle that I didn't think was sexy. I tried to hike my leg up into a really flattering position and fell over, landing directly on the iron I had used on the little black dress just moments before, which was still scalding hot. Now I had a burn the shape of an iron on my ass and not one sexy photo to send.

Mission aborted. I decided Body-Wrap Lady was good for losing some bloat, but from here on out I'd ignore any other advice she offered up.

A few days before I was set to take off to see Baseball Player, I once again stopped hearing from him. In my mind, at this point, he should've been more flirtatious, more attentive, knowing that I was flying there the next week. Ugh, why was this silent thing happening *again*? Boyfriends you've never met or had an actual conversation with can be so unreliable!

I decided he must have met someone. Or he'd changed his mind. I went into my good friend and coworker Jen Kirkman's office and told her everything. I had to fill her in from the top, but she's a quick learner. Neither of us could really figure out what was happening, but Jen suggested I not text him to find out; she suggested I wait to hear from him, then she promised me that if I didn't hear from him by the morning of the day I was supposed to go, she'd go with me, and we'd make a girls' weekend out of it.

"I have miles on Virgin, I can book a flight last-minute and we'll go and have fun."

She is such a good friend. I still felt anxious and oddly a little sad, but at least even if the worst-case scenario happened, my nonrefundable suite at the Four Seasons wouldn't remain empty all weekend.

Friday morning, the day I was supposed to leave, there was still no word from Baseball Player. I still didn't want to text him because I felt like at this point, he knew the plan, seemed excited about the plan, encouraged the plan, and was just being fucking rude.

Jen was just about to book her flight when I got a text from him: "What time do you get in?"

Jen logged off the Virgin America website and we both let out a huge sigh of relief (although she would have gone with me in a heartbeat, I doubt the idea of having to nurse me through a weekend of drinking away the pain of being blown off and trying to wrestle my phone from me every time I wanted to drunk-text him about how he was a big jerk sounded like a lot of fun to her). It's amazing how I let a whole week of anxiety go out the window just because I got one simple text.

Now I was ready to go. I had lost a few pounds and several hundred dollars, but I felt decent about how I looked naked and therefore the money was well spent. That afternoon, I boarded my flight to San Francisco with a carry-on bag full of cute clothes, sexy underwear, and an expensive body exfoliant that Body-Wrap Lady threw in for good luck.

The flight to San Francisco from Los Angeles is barely over an hour, but I managed to down four cocktails. The flight attendant looked both alarmed and impressed.

When I arrived at my hotel, I received a text from Baseball Player asking if I was at my hotel yet. It was Friday night, and my plan was to rest up, go to his game Saturday afternoon, then enjoy a nice evening on the town with him Saturday night.

"I'm here!" I told him. "Can't wait to see you tomorrow."

"Well, what are you doing tonight?" he asked. "I might need a cuddle partner [winking smiley face]."

"Oh, I figured you'd be busy tonight. Where did you want to meet?"

"My hotel room."

This threw me for a loop. I didn't think I'd see him Friday night; I knew he had a game that night followed by a day game

Saturday. Didn't he need to rest? Why would he want to get together with me for the first time ever at eleven p.m. on a Friday night?

*Oh.*

In a panic, I called Tara and then she dialed in Stephanie (Tara is the only one of us who knows how to connect a three-way call).

"So you see him tonight," they explained. "What's the big deal?"

"I don't know! I'm not mentally ready!" I yelled at them while I stood naked in front of my hotel bathroom mirror, checking to see if any new cellulite had erupted below my ass on the flight in. "If I see him tonight it'll be at like eleven p.m. and he has an early day tomorrow. I thought our first time hanging out would be different. You know: dinner, drinks, some talking and laughing . . . then sex after that." I peered in closer at what I was pretty sure was a new dimple and grabbed my tub of FatGirlSlim, a cream that supposedly makes cellulite disappear but clearly doesn't, however I still use it because why not?

"Okay, well, now you can cut right to the sex! Who likes to have sex after dinner, anyway?" Tara said as I massaged the non-miracle cream directly under my ass.

"True. But he wants me to meet him in his hotel room. That seems like a weird place to meet for the first time, doesn't it?"

"Not for a *Major League Baseball player*," Stephanie yelled.

"You're breathing funny," Tara said. "You aren't massaging that stupid cream onto your body again, are you? There's no way that stuff works."

"Of course I'm not, Tara, Jesus," I said as I rubbed another layer onto my belly because, again, why not? "I don't know; I feel like if I go see him tonight we won't hang out tomorrow night."

The girls told me that seemed silly and I should just go with it. "You're already there—maybe this is even better! Your body wrap may wear off before tomorrow," Tara said.

They were right. I had already put so much into this; why not just let it play out however he wanted it to?

On the way out the door, I noticed I'd developed a large pimple right on my cheek (the cheek on my face, you guys). *What the fuck? Really? I'm fucking thirty-seven.* I did my best to cover it and prayed Baseball Player wouldn't be looking at anything above my neck.

So at eleven thirty p.m. I knocked on his hotel room door, which was ajar.

"Come in," Baseball Player yelled out.

I realized up to that point I hadn't ever really heard him talk.

I walked into his room to find him snuggled up in bed, under the covers, watching ESPN.

*Oh my God, he's even cuter in person.*

He motioned for me to come lie next to him, so I did. My heart was racing. *What the fuck am I doing?* I slowly took off my shoes, with my head turned just so to hide the pimple, hoping he'd notice the cute outfit that I'd labored over for three hours before it came flying off. (Cute top, tight jeans, and motorcycle boots. Hello?! What says "laid-back cool girl" more than that?) He didn't notice.

He pulled me close to him and put my head on his shoulder. He apologized for ESPN's being on.

"Oh, that's okay, I watch it all the time."

"I'm super hungover from last night," he told me. "Some of us went out and I've felt like shit all day."

"You can play baseball hungover?" I marveled at this like it was a serious talent.

He smiled. "Let's watch a movie."

*A movie? Okay. Maybe we are going to just hang out tonight. Maybe my plan is still intact and drinks and dinner tomorrow night would be next,* then *we will do it . . . just like I planned.*

I'm not sure why, in my head, putting sex off for one more day made me look less slutty, but let's not try to rationalize a horny and slightly lonely thirty-seven-year-old woman's thoughts when there's a hot Baseball Player involved . . . deal?

Together we selected a movie, but that was really the only conversation we were having. Other than that, he was pretty quiet. It was weird . . . we didn't know each other. But at the same time, it felt like we did; it was kind of awesome. Or so I thought. It's very easy to rationalize awkward silence as some kind of comfortableness when trying to romanticize a situation you've built up in your head.

The movie-ordering feature wasn't working, so I called down to the front desk. The clerk confirmed what room I was in, then said, "So . . . are you with the baseball team?"

I laughed. "Yes, yes I am."

When I hung up Baseball Player asked me what was so funny. I told him the guy asked me if I was "with the baseball team." "It sounded kind of accusatory," I giggled.

He giggled, too, but he didn't quite seem to know why.

We watched the movie in its entirety. I can't remember the name of it now or what it was about. My adrenaline had taken over, and I couldn't focus on anything but trying to see the pimple on my cheek out of the corner of my eye.

Once the movie ended, he turned his face toward mine and laid one on me.

*Okay, maybe we are going to have sex tonight.* I could hear Steph and Tara in my mind: "Just go with it." So I did. (Just to be clear, I didn't continue to hear their voices during the sex.)

I won't lie; it was enjoyable. No fireworks went off and no bells sounded, but everything felt nice and everything was working properly. There was only one problem: he was on top of me the whole time. No, that wasn't the problem, although I prefer to be on top (sorry, Mom, I should have told you to skip this chapter).

The problem was, he was wearing a gold chain and it kept hitting me in the chin. I tried to maneuver my head around the chain, but there was no dodging it. Then I tried to let him know that his jewelry choice was kind of getting in the way of my completely enjoying myself by subtly jerking my head from side to side. He probably just thought I had a tic or something, because he didn't seem to catch on and continued pounding me while his necklace continued pounding me in the face. Eventually, I took my index finger and pressed the offending accessory up against his chest and kept it there until we both finished.

At least we *both* finished.

Afterward, he got up and went to the bathroom. I then took my turn, threw some more concealer on the pimple, and came back to find him once again snuggled up under the covers. He pulled me in again and fell asleep. No talking.

I figured he did have an early game tomorrow and he needed his rest, so I let him have it. I, however, lay there with my eyes wide open, unable to fall asleep. I was trying to figure out how visible my pimple would be in the light of the morning. There was also some sort of band playing on the street below that was so loud that at one point I got up to make sure they weren't playing in the hallway. Baseball Player's sleep was affected by neither the noise nor my insomnia.

The next morning he got up, showered, and put on a nice button-down and pants. I marveled at the fact he got dressed up to go to the field. *Who knew?*

We spoke a little, but not much. *Okay, maybe verbal communication just isn't our thing.*

I lay on the bed with my head propped in my hand as my newest maneuver to hide my adult acne. He asked if I wanted to go to the game that day. I said yes and he let me know he'd leave two tickets for me and explained where I should pick them up.

*Two tickets?* I was by myself. I was there to see him. I thought we had discussed that. I didn't have any friends who lived in the city to call last-minute and invite so that I didn't sit there alone like an asshole. But instead of reminding him I was there this weekend to see him and only him, I just said:

"Perfect! One of my girlfriends will come with me." Then, to cover for postgame when he and I would meet up again and my friend wouldn't be with me because she didn't actually exist, I said, "But she has a kid so she has to go home right after the game."

Now not only did I have a fake friend joining me for the game, my fake friend had a fake baby.

I thanked him for the tickets, wished him a good game, and headed for the hotel elevators. As I got on, so did a couple, whom I immediately recognized as one of the other players for his team and that player's wife (I saw her giant wedding ring, there was no missing it). They looked at me curiously. Well, he did. She looked at me like I was a big fat whore.

*God, this is by far the sluttiest thing I have ever done,* I thought. I was both humiliated and proud.

An hour later, as I was getting super cute for my new boyfriend's baseball game, I decided none of it mattered. He wouldn't see me at the game; I knew where the players' guests sat. He'd never even know I was there alone.

I arrived at the stadium and picked up my tickets. They were there waiting, with my name spelled correctly and everything. That made me happy, although all he really had to do to get that right was look at my Twitter handle. The envelope read "guest of Baseball Player," along with "Family Section."

I took a picture of the envelope and texted it to him along with a note that said, "Family section? Slow down, Tiger." I was proud of my funny little joke; I knew Steph and Tara would be, too.

He wrote back, "Oh, no—that's the section they put all our guests in."

Ugh. He didn't get my funny little joke. This seemed like a pattern.

The game was fun; his team lost but not without his hitting a solo blast in the ninth and scoring his team's only run.

I immediately wrote him after the game: "Nice homer. My friend and I had a blast, thanks for the tickets, she says thanks, too." My fake friend was so polite!

"You're welcome."

I went back to my hotel room and showered. I assumed we'd meet for drinks in a couple of hours, after he got back and got settled from the game. A couple hours later, when I hadn't heard from him, Tara and Steph instructed me to just write him and say, "What's the plan?"

At this point, I had nothing to lose; I had already had sex with him, made up a friend, given her a baby, and failed at getting him to laugh at my jokes, plus I was sporting a tiny bruise on my chin from his gold chain.

Silence. Kind of like after my first bold text to him months ago on opening day, but much, much worse.

I was panicking. I had a long, detailed, three-way phone call with the girls in which we tried to decipher why he was now blowing me off.

"I told you guys I had a feeling if I saw him last night I wouldn't tonight! Why don't I ever listen to my gut? It's so much smarter than my vagina."

We didn't come up with much; they admitted I had been right, which was at least one saving grace, and encouraged me to go to the hotel bar, have some fun, and make the most of it. After all, I had come there to have sex with a *Major League Baseball player* and I had, they reminded me.

"Yeah, what a conquest," I said sarcastically, thanked them for being so supportive while I cried into the phone, and hung up.

I tried to shake off my humiliation and went down to the hotel bar. I ordered a giant hamburger and fries, no longer concerned about what I looked like naked, and drank five martinis. I then went back up to my room to watch TV and feel sorry for myself. At about ten p.m., I got a text.

"WTF! I just woke up!" Baseball Player wrote.

My embarrassment suddenly turned to rage, which is a

much more fun place to come from. "Whatever," I replied. Fuck it; he wasn't exactly a wordsmith either.

"I'm serious! Look!" he wrote, and attached was a photo of him in his hotel bed.

*God, he is so cute*, I thought. Then I spotted the gold chain in the photo and got annoyed again.

"I don't have time for this," I wrote back.

"What do u mean? [frowny face]"

I didn't respond. I was over it. He knew I'd flown up there to see him; that was the whole plan in the first place. I also knew he was telling the truth; he'd fallen asleep. But if someone really wants to see you, they probably will put more effort into staying awake. I know; I aim high.

Quite frankly, based on our correspondence thus far, I had determined he probably wasn't even smart enough to be mean. He was just tired and worse . . . thoughtless. Or that's what I decided, anyway. I don't even know if it's fair to call him thoughtless; for all he knew I was fine and dandy, out having a lovely night with another one of my fake friends.

I fell asleep, woke up the next day, and hauled my bloated ass back to L.A. Maybe he wasn't at fault; after all, I had set myself up for this. My communication with him was just a bunch of text messages. I flew to San Francisco to have sex with him. I couldn't really expect him to garner a bunch of respect for my time or me. We both wanted to do it with each other and we had. How was he supposed to know that along the way, I had spent thousands of dollars?

When I landed back in L.A., the first e-mail I saw was from 1800Flowers.com. "Send something nice to someone you care about today," it read.

*"How many fucking times do I have to unsubscribe from this?"* I yelled, louder than expected. I looked up to see a plane full of people staring at me. Oh well, at least it wasn't a hotel elevator . . .

## Weekend Get-Away from Me

After the Baseball Player incident, I attempted to move forward in my dating life with more realistic goals—like not dating a baseball player *or* anyone I met on a social networking site.

I met a guy, Alex, via Facebook (oh, I only hit one of those goals, but at least it's progress), who worked in the business side of sports. I'd like to clarify what I mean by that, but I can't—not because I'm trying to protect anybody, but because I have no idea. I knew his name, I knew he was successful, and I knew he worked in sports, but that's all the information I was ever able to come up with, even after we met. And after you've been talking to someone for a certain length of time, asking them what they do for a living is just awkward. I have this same issue with my sister. I know she has a job, I know where it is, and I know that she's really, really good at it. But if a nuclear bomb were about to go off and the only way to stop it was for me to tell the guy with his finger on the button my sister's job title, we'd all be fucked.

Alex and I started a little dialogue that, much like my conversations with Baseball Player, eventually led to an exchange of each other's phone numbers. Our initial chatting was something along the lines of: "Oh hey, cool that you are so into sports, so am I," and "I've seen you on TV, you're funny" (always bonus points for a guy who notes that I'm hilarious), then gradually progressed from there. It wasn't a quick cut to flirting or talking about shirts ending up on the floor like my previous social networking affair. In fact, I wasn't even sure that he was flirting with me at all. I just thought maybe he thought I was cool and wanted to make a new friend. This is an issue I have had my entire life. I always assume a guy is not flirting with me and just wants a new BFF, then all of a sudden their penis is inside me and I'm like, "Oh, you didn't want to just go to the mall?" Which is always a relief, because I hate malls.

What I did know from my texting conversations with Alex (I understand a gentleman should offer to call, but when they do I say, "Nope, text is good," because I hate talking on the phone) was that he was handsome and charismatic and seemed to have a really good sense of humor—unlike most of the other men in his field (whatever that was). And much like me, he traveled a lot for work. So one night when we were innocently texting as usual, he suggested that I come to Chicago the following week—because he would be there, not because he just thought I needed more deep-dish pizza in my life. This was the moment I figured out that he had been flirting with me . . . or if he hadn't been before he *definitely* was now. I think. Right?

As had become the norm, I was going to be on the road doing stand-up the very same weekend he was suggesting I come to Chicago and have what I assumed was hot, dirty hotel sex. Why does sex always feel so much dirtier—in the good way—in a hotel? Even my married friends agree that when they have sex in a hotel it feels so much more exciting than at home. I guess it just makes it feel like you're doing something that you shouldn't be doing. Or maybe I just get really turned on by the thought of room service and fresh towels.

"I'm going to be out of town that weekend, but unfortunately not in Chicago," I texted in response to Alex.

"Bummer," he replied. "It would've been great to get to actually meet you."

I'd almost forgotten we hadn't even met yet. We had now been friendly texting for a couple of months but we hadn't met in person, which was kind of weird because he only lived about forty-five minutes away from where I lived, but we both traveled a lot, so I guess he figured meeting up in another city was the only way we'd ever actually meet.

"Well, hopefully we can figure out another time for that . . . ," I texted. As much as I am gone for work, I find that after I meet a man I'm interested in, once I'm out of town and unavailable to see him, he decides that I'm *not* interested in him and the whole thing is over before it even starts. So I did my best to let Alex know that I wanted this "meeting" to happen.

"Definitely," he replied.

Mission accomplished.

During this time, I had been working really hard on the television show based on my book that I'd sold to NBC. Alex took a lot of interest in that aspect of my life, and I appreciated that. Not to say the other people in my life, like my friends, family, and coworkers, didn't take an interest in it; of course they did. But it was nice to be talking to someone who didn't do what I did yet was very interested in what I did. And vice versa for him. I mean, he didn't know I didn't know exactly what he did, but he knew I listened when he talked (texted) about it, so that was good. I assume it's like this for everyone, regardless of their job; meeting someone who in no way is in your field of work is refreshing and exhilarating. It brings new life into your own career for you—suddenly someone is truly interested in what you do, which in turn brings new excitement to it for you. So both personally and professionally, Alex was making me feel interesting and wanted. I liked Alex.

My show didn't end up going any further than NBC's buying the script, which needless to say was incredibly disappointing. But it's really hard to sell a show, much harder to get them to shoot the pilot, and even ridiculously harder to get it on the air. So after getting really hammered at noon the day I found out the bad news and waking up at six o'clock p.m. on my bed wearing only a pair wedges, I picked myself up and moved on. You have to allow yourself a day of mourning, but then you have to get over it. About four years previous to selling that show to NBC, I was bartending and barely making ends meet. I knew I had come far and I knew that things could always turn on a dime as long as you never quit trying to reach your goal.

"I'm so sorry, I know how hard you were working on that," Alex texted me when I told him the news about my show.

"Thank you," I responded, very touched/horny that he genuinely seemed to care.

"So what's next?" he asked.

"Next I come up with another idea and sell that."

"I like your motivation. It's sexy," he replied.

"I just drank a bottle of wine and now I'm watching *Road House*—is that sexy?" I asked. Sometimes when I'm nervous I try to be funny. I mean, I really was drunk and watching *Road House*, but I probably could've come up with something sexier than the truth.

"It is if you're thinking of yourself as Kelly Lynch and me as Patrick Swayze . . ."

*Oh, it is on!* I thought. No doubt he was flirting with me now! *HE COMPARED US TO KELLY LYNCH AND PATRICK SWAYZE.*

"I certainly am," I wrote back coyly. "But not the part where he rips the guy's throat out. That's not sexy."

Silence.

If I didn't get into comedy I could've been a professional mood-killer.

"No, it isn't," he wrote back about thirty minutes later.

*Note to self: stop trying to be funny or you're going to die alone.*

The next day, I was texting with my friend Jackie and I told her what Alex had said about *Road House*.

"He asked you to meet him in Chicago, and you think the *Road House* reference is when he really made his move?"

"Well, that's like the most romantic couple in the history of cinema," I explained.

"Patrick Swayze played a bouncer in that movie."

"Bouncers can't be romantic?"

"He ripped someone's throat out with his bare hands."

"I specifically told him I was not referring to that part of the movie, Jackie. I'm not a moron."

"I feel like you have weird ideas of what is romantic . . ."

"Me? You and Brandon go camping all the time, which, in my opinion, is something you suggest when you want to punish the other person."

"Ha ha, fine. I'm just saying, I think it's pretty clear this guy wants in your pants so you don't have to get hung up on a movie reference. Instead, why don't you set a time where you can actually meet him and get some penetration? When was the last time you had sex?"

"Ugh, like, eight months ago. I'm basically a virgin again. I'm afraid it's going to close up like an earring hole does when you forget to put earrings in for too long."

"Can that happen?"

"I think so."

"Well, in that case I better go find Brandon, it's been like a week. Wait, Alex lives here, right? Why can't you just meet up with him in town?"

"He lives north, like an hour away."

"That is a little bit closer than Chicago. Why doesn't he just drive to meet you? Wait . . . are you sure this guy isn't married?"

"Huh?"

"I'm just saying, it's kind of weird. If he really wanted to meet you, it seems like he could've by now."

"No, he isn't married. He can't be, he texts me all the time. And he certainly didn't say he was married."

"Did you ask?"

"Was I supposed to? That seems like something people let you know right away."

"Well, not all people. Just make sure. Something sounds off."

I wasn't sure. And now that Jackie had mentioned it, things did seem kind of weird. But seriously, is that how life was now? Had I been out of the normal dating game for so long that I didn't get the memo that when someone asks you out on a date you have to first ask them to specify whether or not they're married? Jesus.

Clearly the easiest way to get an answer to this question would be to ask Alex whether or not he was married. But I decided to try to get an answer on my own. I had two reasons for not wanting to flat-out ask him: (1) If he was not, he would probably think I was a little insane for asking that out of the blue. (2) If he was, and hadn't told me yet, who was to say he'd tell me the truth now?

So I decided to launch my own investigation. Unfortunately, his Facebook page was simply for work and revealed nothing about his personal life. So I typed his name plus "wife" into Google. Within seconds, I had my answer.

According to Google, Alex was, in fact, married. So easy to find out that way, you'd think I would have done that before, wouldn't you? Well, trust me, when I meet someone now, it's the first thing I do.

Since Alex isn't in the public eye, I wasn't able to get a ton of information. What I did get was a photo of him and his wife (who was very lovely) at an event about two years prior. I immediately called Jackie with my revelation.

"Ugh, I knew something was fishy," she sighed.

"The problem is, all I could find was a picture of them at an event a couple of years ago. Maybe he's divorced, which would mean he's single, which would mean he isn't doing anything wrong."

"The only way to find out is to ask him," Jackie said. "You have to ask."

I knew she was right. It seemed so easy to just pick up my phone and send him a text that said: "Hey, quick question, are you married?" But it wasn't that easy. I liked Alex. I know I hadn't met him in person yet, but we had been talking for a few months at this point and I *felt* like I knew him. Every relationship in my life was being maintained via text, so I guess the one I'd formed with Alex didn't seem that weird to me. He was smart, funny, and interesting. And he felt the same way about me.

Although I was incredibly grateful that my career was finally growing into what I'd always dreamed it would be, I was traveling all the time, and I'd be lying if I said I wasn't starting to feel the void of not having some romance in my life. I'd come home from a weekend on the road to unwind and find myself having one too many drinks on my balcony and staring at my cat. In short, I was pretty fucking lonely.

I lay in bed that night, phone in hand, trying to figure out the best way to get the answer to what seemed like such a simple question. I didn't want Alex to turn out to be an asshole. I'd worked so hard to not date assholes, to not settle. And if I was going to hang out with an asshole, it needed to be for sex and a good story, like with Baseball Player. Alex's turning out to be married wasn't a good story, especially since I actually liked him.

I woke up the next morning, my phone on the floor next to me. I guess I'd overthought myself to sleep. When I picked it up, there was a text from Alex waiting for me.

"I'm going to be in Seattle next weekend for work. Meet me there? I have the whole day and night free on Saturday."

Seattle made me think of those stupid sunflowers I'd sent Baseball Player and I made a mental note to unsubscribe from 1800Flowers.com again. Seriously, I was still getting e-mails from them.

"Actually, I'm free next weekend," I replied. "Sounds fun."

I know what you're thinking. Why didn't I say, "Sure, I'll be there, as long as you don't have a wife, LOL!"? But I wasn't ready to ask him yet. I wanted to spend one day fantasizing about a romantic weekend in Seattle. I'd ask him tomorrow.

Three days later, I still hadn't asked Alex the big question. I booked my hotel, I booked my plane ticket, and I bought a new outfit (but I didn't book any body wraps, so that's progress). I was forging ahead with the idea that the man who was constantly texting me and had asked me on more than one occasion to meet him in other cities was single, as presented. But I couldn't get the image of that photo stupid Google shoved in my face out of my head. So I decided it was time to find out.

"Oh, hey, I was thinking: I'm performing here in L.A. next month, you should come down for it. I can put you and your wife on the list."

I know that sounds like a very strange way to ask, but it was all I could come up with. I figured if he wasn't married, he'd say, "Wife? I don't have a wife! I'm divorced!" Then I could say, "I know, I was just joking! Ha ha." And if he was married, he certainly wasn't going to ask me how I found out. (Look, I never claimed to have a degree in logic.)

"Sounds good," he responded.

My stomach sank. I was four days away from meeting this man in Seattle and he had just confirmed, via text, that he was married. And not only did he not ask me how I figured it out, he didn't even address it. Did he just assume that I knew all along? And if so, why? I stared at his text for like forty minutes, completely stumped as to how to respond to it, or if I should even respond at all. I mean, I guess I had my answer. Didn't I?

I came up with various scenarios in my head: He might be separated. But that didn't make sense because if he was, he probably would have said, "I'm separated," instead of, "Sounds good." He might be in a green card marriage, but that didn't make sense because if he was, he probably would have said, "I am married, but I just did it to help out a friend in need of a green card," instead of, "Sounds good." He might be a widower, but that didn't make sense because if he was, he probably would have said, "I'll just need one ticket to your show since my wife is dead," instead of, "Sounds good." The only scenario that made sense was that he was married, that he didn't tell me, that he knew I'd found out, and that he was busted. So all he really had to say for himself was: "Sounds good."

I didn't hear from Alex the rest of that day and honestly I figured I wouldn't be hearing from him again now that the jig was up. But the next day, I got a text from him that said, "Seattle . . . tick, tock. Can't wait."

I was confused and angry. Did I misread this entire thing all along? Did he just want to be friends and therefore my mention of his marriage didn't change anything for him? The thing is, I know a lot of married people and they certainly don't make new friends of the opposite sex and then have said friends meet them in other cities on the weekends.

An hour later, another text came through from Alex. "Sorry I didn't write you last night, someone was next to me most of the evening."

My stomach sank further. Then I got pissed. For months there had been no mention of a wife or a marriage, but when I found out and I let him know I'd found out, now he was all open about it? Did he think I'd think that was awesome? And as for the texting-at-night thing, where the fuck was she sitting for the past sixteen weeks? Because it didn't seem to be a problem before. I had so many questions but instead of asking them I just stared at my phone. This was becoming a pattern.

The day before I was supposed to leave to meet Alex in Seattle, I got a text from him asking me what time I got in.

"I get in at 4," I replied.

"Great, text me when you land and I'll meet you at your hotel."

I packed my bags that night. I shoved everything to the back of my mind and decided to just meet him in Seattle and get my answers there. Maybe he was in a bad marriage, maybe it was coming to an end. But these weren't questions I felt like I could get answers to via text. I thought his "Sounds good" spoke for itself. The only way for me to know what this was between us and what exactly was going on with his marriage was to go to Seattle and find out. At least that's what I told myself.

I talked to Jackie that night, asking her what I should do.

"I think you should stay in town," she said firmly. "Some of us are going out to Malibu tomorrow for happy hour. Come get drunk and forget about this guy."

"I don't know, Jackie. I want answers. I want to know what he's been thinking this is this whole time."

"Think about it. You probably already know the answer to that."

I lay in bed that night with my eyes open, staring at the ceiling. When my alarm finally went off I'd probably racked up a whole forty-seven minutes of sleep.

I got up, put a couple more things in my bag, and zipped it shut. Then I made myself some breakfast, sat on my balcony, and stared at my cat. *So apparently I'm doing this in the mornings now, too?* I thought as I contemplated completing the familiar routine with a cocktail. It was nine o'clock in the morning; I don't even drink at nine o'clock in the morning when I'm on vacation . . . I always wait until at least ten a.m. so that it's double digits on the clock when I start. It's called being responsible.

After about an hour of staring at Mischief, I grabbed my phone and texted Alex.

"I've decided to stay home this weekend. Sorry."

"Whatever," he replied.

Not the most satisfying response, but I had already come to the conclusion that I was never going to be satisfied with any response I got from him. I knew what I needed to know: Alex was married. It didn't matter if he was happily married, unhappily married, in a green card marriage, or in an open marriage: none of those were things I wanted in my life. If I thought I felt lonely now, imagine how lonely it would be to have a married boyfriend. I deserved better. And yes, I figured this all out while staring at my cat. He's like a Buddha, if Buddhas jumped on your chest in the middle of the night and coughed up hair balls.

I unpacked my bag and got dressed to go to Malibu. I'd been missing my friends and now I was finally home for a weekend to spend time with them. That was what I needed.

At around five o'clock that evening, while I sat at a table with four of my closest girlfriends, drinking mai tais and laughing, I got a text from Alex.

"Are you here yet?" he asked.

*Wait, what?*

"I told you earlier, I'm not coming."

"Seriously? I thought you were joking. I'm so disappointed."

I can't lie; part of me was extremely satisfied that he'd sent his earlier response because he didn't think I was being serious. And another part of me was even more satisfied that I had disappointed him—the way he had disappointed me.

Another text came through: "I really am disappointed," he said.

"Sounds good," I replied.

## It Ain't Over till the Cat Lady Sings

So I had a cat, Mischief, for sixteen years. The same cat—not a whole bunch of different cats over that span of time. I mean, I'm not insane.

Having a cat didn't do much for my dating life. You see, when you're single and you have a dog, people think you're cool and you love to hike. When you're single and you have a cat, people think you're a loser and you love to watch the Lifetime network. I would just like to clarify that both of those stereotypes are 100 percent accurate. The only time I like to hike is when I'm filling out the "activities" portion of an online dating profile; in reality, I prefer spin classes. Sorry, I've seen a lot more chubby hikers than I have spinners. And if the Lifetime network didn't exist, then as far as I'm concerned, neither should Sundays.

Anyway, the struggle of being a single woman and owning a cat is real. However, I didn't purposely go out and get my cat. I didn't put on my Shape-up Skechers one day and head out to the cat store. I inherited my cat from a boyfriend who died in a car accident. But I'm not going to get into that (again).

I realize that some people disagree when you say having a pet is similar to having a child. Well guess what: I cared for Mischief for sixteen years. He relied on me for food, water, and shelter. I took him to get his shots. I cared for him when he was sick and I cleaned up after him when he pooped. Plus, cats don't grow out of it and start using the toilet like kids— like *most* kids—do. I mean, I have seen a couple of YouTube videos with cats using the toilet but my point is, having a pet is similar to having a child except before they can grow up, go to college, and start paying you back for all the hard work you put in, they die.

I've never liked parents who act like their kids are awesome all the time, so I'm not going to do that when I talk about my cat: my cat was an asshole. He had a deep, loud meow that he only let out late at night when I was trying to sleep, but even worse: when I was trying to sleep with a gentleman caller. I don't know if it was some sort of protective instinct because he knew I used to date his dad or if he just had some sort of beef with my having company in general, but it usually ended with the guy saying, *"What the fuck is wrong with your cat?"* then leaving because he had to "get a good night's sleep," which for the first several years I always knew was bullshit because most of the guys I had sex with in my early twenties were unemployed.

My cat also fancied himself quite the foodie. Although he would eat his *perfectly fit-for-cats* cat food all day long, the second I broke out any food for myself, he would approach me in a manner that seemed harmless, then out of nowhere his paw would come up and swipe my entire meal. He just took food out of my hand. It didn't matter what it was either. He wasn't one of those cats who thought he wanted your food, then once he got it realized that he didn't. He always really, really wanted it. He obviously preferred when I was hungover because he'd get a delicious meal like a Quarter Pounder or Taco Bell. But he'd pretty much eat anything. One time I left a bag of Ruffles open on my couch while I went to grab water (Ruffles are very salty) and came back to find half of his body *inside* the bag. When I pulled him out, he was eating a Ruffle and looking at me like I was the asshole. I swear I've even seen him eat sauerkraut. He didn't give a shit what it was, he just wanted food.

This was a huge date killer when someone was over and I cooked—well, ordered Chinese food. After Mischief had made off with half of the guy's lo mein and an egg roll, I'd apologize and lock the little bastard (the cat, not the guy) in my bedroom so we could finish our meal in peace and play that super-fun "in bed" game with our fortune cookies. Mischief never went quietly, though. He'd meow in this deep, throaty tone that my friend Sarah Tilley dubbed his "Barry White" and stick his paw under the door to rattle it. It was like living with a lion. I'd just turn the volume up on the TV louder and louder in an attempt to drown him out while my dinner guest looked at me in horror, asking if I was sure my cat was okay.

"He's fine," I'd assure him. "I think he's just possessed with the spirit of his previous owner."

"Um, what was that?" the guy would ask.

"This guy I was dating. He died while we were dating and I kept the cat. Can you pass the fried rice?"

"He died while you were dating?"

"Yeah, but it was a long time ago, it's fine. It's not like I killed him or anything!" I'd say and laugh.

Those nights Mischief let me sleep in peace, because I would inevitably end up spending the rest of the night alone.

Now, I don't want you to think my cat sat around eating fast food all day, because then you'll think he wasn't healthy and I gave him diabetes. At least that's what happened one night when I made a joke about his being a loud fat-ass when I was on *Chelsea Lately*. Here's the actual e-mail I received the day after the show (the typos belong to the person who wrote it):

> *Sarah:*
>
> *Why get a cat if you're not going to take good care of it and learn how to care for it properly? It's obese because of your stupidity. It didn't do it by itself.*
>
> *Animals food needs to be restricted just as for any human. Look at Chuy! Look at the people who can't even get out of bed! You're doing the same fucking thing to a precious animal who can't change what YOU do to it!!!*

*Food 24/7 also creates crystals in the kidneys which block the urethra.*

*Why don't you EDUCATE yourself about an animal BEFORE you decide to get one, instead of abusing the poor thing.*

*You need to take the cat to the Humane Society and get it proper care since you don't give a shit*

*Fucking cunt. You should be arrested for animal abuse.*

*Sad thing is. . . . . you'll probably make "jokes" about it instead of being a caring, compassionate, loving person.*

*Just shows what a pathetic excuse for a human being you are.*

*Wilson*

Nice, huh?
And here's my reply:

*Dear Wilson,*
*First of all, is that true about the urethra? Because I also eat food and I'm almost positive I have a urethra and I never want anything that's not in liquid form coming out of it.*

*Next: I've had my cat for sixteen years, and he's as healthy and happy as can be. The vet says his weight is normal, but thanks for your input! He's also very loud, which I did make a joke about because I'm a fucking comedian—or as you called it, a "cunt."*

*Oh, and I didn't "go get" a cat, I inherited my cat from a boyfriend who died suddenly and tragically in a car accident and I have taken loving care of him ever since. That's a true story! You can read all about that and more in my* New York Times *bestseller* Life as I Blow It.

*PS: Thanks for watching the show!!!!*

*Sarah*

In reality, yes, my cat was a pain in the ass, and yes, he enjoyed stealing food. But I took really good care of him. I mean, he lived, nice and healthy, for sixteen years. I monitored his human-food intake. He only got a bite here and there. You think I'd let *anyone* eat all of my Big Mac? Never. I've ended relationships over shit like that.

Mischief also opened cabinets in my hallway in the middle of the night with his man paws; when I'd get up to go to the bathroom or get a glass of water, I'd bang into them and wake up with giant bruises on my knee (bruises are never good unless they are the kind you get from adult fun time). But he did some really cool things, too, like curl up on my lap when I would watch TV. He loved baseball and *General Hospital*, just like me. Sometimes he would sleep on my chest, which can be creepy when you wake up but for the most part is pretty awesome. *He* was awesome. And I took good care of him because as fucking annoying as he was at times, I loved him. I assume my parents feel the same way about me.

So when he started to act differently I took him to the vet. He was constipated—we shared many of the same issues—and not eating much. The "not eating" was what really worried me: that's like me telling my friends I don't want any alcohol; they'd know something was way off.

The vet ran some tests and told me Mischief had kidney failure. She said it's what most older cats eventually develop. It's terminal, but there are some things you can do for them to make them comfortable enough to live happily for a while longer. The first one of those "things" the vet told me was that I was going to need to administer an IV to my cat daily.

"Excuse me?"

She took me into a room and showed me how to do it. How to stick a big fat needle into his back—that he didn't really seem to feel, but whatever, she was sticking a needle in my fucking cat! I wanted to punch her in the face. She kept it there while a certain amount of liquid something poured into his body and apparently hydrated him. I cried while she did it and I cried when she told me I was going to have to do it.

"Fuck that noise," I told her. "Can't I bring him in here and have you guys do it?"

"Sure," she said. "But most cats don't enjoy going to the vet and it would be easier on you to do it at home. You'd have to bring him in here every day for the rest of his life."

She was right. Mischief hated going to the vet. I used to have to go downstairs, crack open the door on his little carrier, and position it just so, so that when I got him downstairs

I could shove him in it before he had the chance to realize what was happening. Otherwise, the second he saw it he'd dart under the bed and out of my reach. Then when I finally did get him in it, he'd do his deep loud meow, but with an extra tone of misery added in that made me feel like I was an animal abuser.

"Fuck that noise," I repeated. "I'll see you every day for the rest of his life."

After three days of taking him to the vet, both of us crying the whole way (I realized then that I also sound like Barry White when I'm upset), I knew I was going to have to learn to do it myself.

So, I sucked it up. The vet explained to me that we'd both get used to it and soon enough I'd be able to administer the IV painlessly. I thanked her and told her that she was probably pretty wrong about that.

So every morning, I woke up, went into the kitchen, hung the IV bag onto a hanger on a cabinet, pulled my cat into my arms, and stuck a needle in him. I've never felt so single.

The vet was right, though; we both got used to it. I think Mischief knew it made him feel better. He even got to where he was purring when I'd do it. I assume this is the same kind of bonding that happens with heroin addicts.

A week or so later I took him in for a follow-up, and the next day the vet called to let me know that he probably didn't have much longer. She said to keep doing what I was doing, gave me like four more medications, and told me what to look out for so that when it was time to let him go I would "know."

So now not only was I jamming an IV into him, I was trying to get him to swallow various pills—cats love having pills tossed down their throats—and putting some weird shit into his food. At this point it felt like I was taking care of my dying grandfather.

It was all getting to be a lot; he had some good days where he felt okay, but the bad days started to take over until one day I found him peeing right beside the litter box. Not inside it—beside it. The vet told me this was one of those "signs." I don't know why they do that, I just know she said he would and he did. When I found him in action, he looked up at me—I expected him to feel bad about peeing on the floor, so I was ready to let him know that I knew it wasn't his fault. Instead he just looked at me like, "What? I'm peeing," and sauntered off. Even near death he could still be an asshole, and I appreciated that about him.

I let the vet know what was happening and she softly suggested it was time. She said that often people hold on to pets for too long because they don't want to let them go, but in reality it's unfair to the animal, who can't make decisions for himself. Although, I kind of felt like Mischief made the decision for himself the day he walked by me and pooped right next to my foot. He was letting me know it was time. Five minutes after that, he lay on my chest and purred. I was afraid he was going to poop again right then and there, which, just for the record, is something I've never let any man do. But he didn't. He just lay there so I'd know he still loved me. I loved him, too—so I had to do what was right.

I've never had to put a pet to sleep before; I grew up in Arkansas. Most of our pets got run over by some jackass going too fast on a dirt road. My stepdad always buried them in our pasture (yeah, we had a pasture—I'm very worldly) and that was that. So this was all very new to me.

"I'VE NEVER DONE THIS BEFORE, I DON'T EVEN KNOW WHAT TO DO," I wailed to the vet. God bless that woman, that can't be an easy job, but she was so nice and patient with me. She explained that I could bring him in and they could do it there or she could come to my home and do it there. I didn't even know they did that.

*"THAT ONE, I WANNA DO THAT ONE,"* I sobbed. I couldn't imagine driving him to his death—it seemed so mob-like. This other way he could pass away at home like a respected senior citizen should.

I have some pretty great friends, I have to say. The night the vet was coming to put him down, three of them came over. We drank wine, shared silly memories about Mischief (they've known him a long time, too), and gave him tons of love. He was pretty stoked about all the attention; he perked up and was like, *"What's up, ladies?"* taking full advantage.

When the vet knocked on my door, we all just stared at each other. The girls offered to let her in but I said I would do it; I could do it. She came up and softly explained to me the quick procedure; she'd give him a shot that he would barely feel to sedate him, then after a couple of minutes, when he was definitely unable to feel anything, she'd give him the shot that would make his little heart stop.

I put him on his favorite blanket in his favorite spot (right next to the refrigerator), and the vet gave him the sedative. He looked at all of us, inquisitive, tired—but he seemed relaxed. He also seemed to know it was time to go—maybe that sounds crazy, but whatever, my cat died, so give me a fucking break.

When she knew he was fully sedated, she gently told me it was time. I started sobbing, harder than I even knew that I could—uncontrollable, childlike sobbing—Barry White in full effect. My friends were crying, too; it was a mess. I nodded to the vet, letting her know to go ahead, and she did. I stared at Mischief the whole time, looking in his eyes, telling him I loved him and that I was so sorry I couldn't do anything else to make him feel better. I waited for his eyes to close but they never did, then the vet explained to me that they wouldn't, which was pretty fucking creepy. And I *swear to God* I saw a tear fall out of the corner of his eye. I *swear*. Later I figured out that it was most likely one of my own tears that landed on his face because, you know, cats can't cry.

After a few minutes, she listened to his heartbeat, looked up at me, and said, "I'm so sorry." Uncontrollable sobbing again. That was it; my little buddy was gone.

I slept with his collar on my wrist for a couple of nights. It made me feel better, except when I'd turn in my sleep and it would jingle and wake me up, which probably sounds annoying but it wasn't too terrible for someone who once had to sleep in an electronic home monitoring bracelet.

To this day, I still feel sad; I come home and he's not at the door waiting for me like he was for sixteen years. I go into my kitchen and he doesn't follow me, screaming at me, letting me know he wants some fucking turkey. I've even put on weight since he's been gone—not because I miss him but because I'm finally able to finish all of my meals myself now. It sucks. Living alone is one thing when you have a pet to care for, but when you lose that pet, there's an emptiness that makes you question your decision to be alone. That said, if you talk about that in public, you just sound like a crazy cat lady. But I won't let it stop me; Mischief deserves more respect than that.

I wanted to tell that story and I guess I wanted to give him a shout-out. I really felt like he earned his own chapter in this book. I did a lot of joking around about him, but obviously, I loved him. You can't really have something for sixteen years and not love it. Except maybe herpes.

## The No-Sunshine State

One weekend I was performing in Fort Lauderdale for the first time, and I was looking forward to some serious sunshine and poolside time during the day. It was March and it was Florida . . . hello, sun!

It rained the entire time.

The comedy club there is part of a complex set way off by itself. There are restaurants and a casino, but once you're there, you're there. And if it's raining, you're fucked.

Due to the rain, "pool" time quickly turned into "sit in my room" time. It easily could've turned into "play blackjack in the casino" time, but gambling during the day makes me feel like a degenerate. Unless of course I'm in Vegas, in which case all bets are off (or on).

The shows were pretty rowdy; in fact, one night a girl in the audience was so obnoxious she ended up getting kicked out. In the process, she also punched the bouncer in the face. Fucking

Florida. Mind you, this all occurred while I was onstage trying to be hilarious—my job is fun, but it isn't always easy.

On the second night, I ended up flirting, from the stage, with a very hot guy in the audience. I do that from time to time, but it's not meant to be taken all that seriously. However, in this case, hot guy took me pretty seriously and waited for me during my book signing after the show. I spotted him in line and started to get kind of nervous; he seemed pretty locked in on me and now that he was up close, I was noticing that he was really ripped—he was basically just a giant pair of biceps.

He kept letting people go around him in line, which was making me more nervous. *Why is he waiting to talk to me?* I wondered. Also, he appeared to be alone, which made me nervous on a different level.

Once the line started to wind down, Hot Ripped Guy came up and handed me a piece of paper.

"That's my number if you wanna get a drink when you're done here, girl." He smiled.

*Girl?* I cringed a little. "So you aren't waiting in line because you want to make a skin suit out of me?" I asked, only half joking.

"I was wondering why you were looking at me so skeptically," he laughed. "I swear you started to sweat as I got closer, but I was hoping that was out of attraction rather than fear."

"It's rude to tell a girl she's sweaty," I declared.

"But you are sweaty."

"Solid point," I laughed as I self-consciously took the number out of his hand, careful not to raise my arm up much in case my armpit sweat was visible. Not only do I sweat when I talk to guys I'm attracted to, which I'm sure is a huge turn-on, but I sweat when I perform. Like, a lot. It's terrible and embarrassing but there's nothing I can do about it, except always wear dark colors or tank tops when I do stand-up . . . or talk to guys . . . or move.

"So are you going to text me when you're done so I can buy you a drink or was that all an act?"

"Oh, it was definitely an act." I smiled. "But that doesn't mean I won't let you buy me a drink."

"Good," he laughed. "I'll expect to hear from you soon."

When Hot Ripped Guy walked away, I noticed that he also had a hot ripped ass.

When I got back to my room later, I stared at Hot Ripped Guy's number for a while. I had never hooked up with a guy from the audience before, and I had never planned to. I may do a lot of dumb things, but work is work, and also, I know what can happen when a woman traveling alone on business invites a strapping young man up to her room. I told you—I watch Lifetime; I don't want to end up in a freezer.

*He seemed pretty harmless . . . and ripped,* I thought. *And there's always a first time for everything, right?*

I sat on the bed in my hotel room for about an hour contemplating texting Hot Ripped Guy. I couldn't decide if it was a good idea or a bad idea, but I was definitely overthinking it. I hadn't had sex for several months at this point and I wasn't sure I wanted to do it now with a stranger at a casino in Florida.

*But all he said was he wanted to buy you a drink; what if he just wants to buy you a drink? That might be nice . . .*

Four hours later I woke up, still in my clothes and still clutching Hot Ripped Guy's phone number. Now it was three o'clock in the morning and I definitely wasn't texting anyone.

The next day I woke up to more rain. Realizing my pool plans were ruined, I picked up Hot Ripped Guy's number. I figured, *Why not see what he's up to since I have nothing to do until my show at eight p.m.? He can still buy me a drink, just in the daylight instead.*

"It's Sarah . . . you still want to buy me a drink?" I texted.

"Wow, your book signing just ended? That's crazy . . ."

"Yeah, my book-signing poster accidentally got switched out with a *Twilight* poster so people thought they were waiting in line for tickets. There were some pretty unhappy campers," I joked. Okay, not my best, I know.

Hot Ripped Guy met me at the pool bar and we sat under the awning in the rain and had a drink. We had a decent conversation, nothing groundbreaking, but I was able to determine that he was mildly intelligent and somewhat funny. I also knew not to expect too much from a hot ripped guy; I've made that mistake before.

After he informed me that his name was "Jayson with a Y," we ran out of things to talk about, so we decided to go gamble. We played a couple hands of blackjack in the crowded casino, where it seemed everyone had gone in order to escape the rain. So I suggested we go get something to eat.

"Let's go to your room and order room service," Hot Ripped Jayson with a Y suggested, smiling.

Clearly he wanted me to have penis for lunch.

I decided that since I hadn't seen a penis in a while, there were worse ideas. So I agreed and we headed up to my room.

I hadn't decided for sure if I was going to have sex with him *and* I really was hungry, so when we got to my room I picked up the phone to order room service. Within seconds, I felt a hand take the phone out of mine and hang it up; next thing I knew Hot Ripped Jayson with a Y had me pressed up against the hotel room door. I didn't even know how he had moved me so quickly; I'm pretty sure I was airborne part of the way but I couldn't really keep track of the details.

"I really need to eat something . . . ," I began to protest, but I didn't mean it. I just felt as though acting like I needed to think about what was about to transpire was the proper thing to do.

"I kind of want to eat something, too," Hot Ripped Jayson with a Y responded in what I think was his attempt at a sexy voice.

I laughed, which he didn't seem to appreciate. But *come on*, who talks like that?

He muffled my giggles with his mouth and suddenly I was pressed up against the hotel window and I was no longer wearing pants. *Is this guy a Ninja?* My room was really high up and it overlooked the pool, but still, my ass was on full display. I peeked over my shoulder and, wait . . . there were a bunch of people down by the pool now. *The sun finally decides to come out, now that I've clearly committed to having intercourse with this guy? Just my luck.*

I tried to wriggle off the window, quietly suggesting we go over to the bed where other people couldn't see us.

"I doubt anyone can see us all the way up here, but if they can it's pretty fucking sexy," Hot Ripped Jayson with a Y responded.

"I don't know if it's all that sexy," I replied as I pictured what my ass must look like smashed against glass by a man three times my size.

"Oh, it's hot, girl, it's hot, girl . . ."

*This guy is super talkative,* I thought. *And I really wish he'd stop calling me "girl."* The sex against the window, the dirty talk, it was all a little much for me considering we'd just met. That stuff usually starts happening once you're comfortable with someone, not after one drink and a couple rounds of black-jack. I once again started to laugh.

"You think this dick is funny, girl?" he asked me as he put my hand right on it.

"What? No! What?" I said, totally embarrassed for both of us that he was talking this way.

"You keep laughing; you think this dick is funny?"

"No, your dick isn't funny. I'm sorry. It's just . . . I'm not used to all this talking, that's all. Maybe less of that and more of the other stuff?" I suggested in what I hoped was a sexy but stern voice.

The more clothes he took off, the hotter I realized his body was, and I really wanted to be able to go through with the sex part of this, but in order to do so I really needed him to shut the fuck up.

Hot Ripped Jayson with a Y spun me around and now it was his bare ass on display for the lovely folks of Fort Lauderdale. I moved my head to the side, which he took as a hint to kiss my neck, but really I was just trying to assess the pool situation. *If we wrap this up quickly, I can still get in some suntanning time,* I thought. Then I noticed that a woman who was probably in her seventies was staring directly up at us.

"Oh my God, I think an old lady just saw us," I yelled.

"Yeah, that's hot . . ."

"It isn't hot, get me away from this window; I can't take it," I demanded.

Hot Ripped Jayson with a Y obeyed and took me over to the bed to have sex like normal people. I relaxed a little now that I was out of these strangers' sight lines and started to enjoy myself. I mean, here was this really hot guy who was into me and now we were going to have sex—I've definitely had worse weekends.

Things proceeded to the stage of intercourse and now I was really starting to enjoy myself.

Then Hot Ripped Jayson with a Y whispered softly into my ear, "Get that dick."

I thought I was getting it, but apparently not.

I ignored him and kept on with what we were doing.

"Get that dick," he whispered again.

"Okay," I whispered back, hoping that would stop him from repeating it.

"Get that dick," he said, louder.

"All right," I replied, also louder.

"Get that dick," he yelled.

I closed my eyes and tried to think about anything I could to keep from laughing. I thought about the old lady who just saw us having sex. I thought about the girl who punched the bouncer in the face. I thought about my dead cat. I tried everything, but I felt myself starting to break.

"Get that dick!" he screamed.

I couldn't take it anymore. "I got it!" I yelled. "Jesus, I got it. Seriously, what the fuck?"

Apparently that did it for him because suddenly it was all over. We separated and I started to laugh, then looked up to see that he was not laughing. *Oh, he's still serious,* I thought.

I got up and got dressed, but within seconds he was pulling at my clothes again.

"What are you doing?" I asked, seriously unsure what he was doing.

"I'm going for round two," he said in his weird sex voice.

"No, I'm still tired from round one," I said as I wriggled away. I really wanted to get to the pool.

"Come on, girl . . ."

"You have to stop calling me 'girl,' I feel like I'm talking to the lead singer of a boy band."

"Ouch," he laughed.

Then it sank in. "Wait, how old are you?" I asked him. That detail hadn't come up before (hey, at least I got his name this time).

"Twenty-seven." He smiled proudly.

"Yeah, that makes more sense now," I mumbled. Good Lord, he was ten years younger than me. I guess some people would have been proud of this fact but it just made me feel dirty(er).

"Look, Jay-son; I like sex a whole bunch, and that was . . . sex . . . ," I said gently, searching for an adjective but coming up with nothing. "But I'm really hungry and I have a show to do tonight, so I think let's just call it a day."

Hot Ripped Jayson with a Y looked dejected. For a second I felt bad but then I remembered that I'd just had sex with him and that if I heard him say, "Get that dick," one more time my head would explode.

"Okay, girl," he said as he kissed me on the forehead and headed for the door.

*He really doesn't listen,* I thought as I waved to him, which I now realize was a totally weird thing to do.

He had told me earlier that he didn't live far from the hotel, which meant he wasn't staying at the hotel, which meant I could now safely go to the pool, order lunch, and get some sun. Alone, just how I like it. *Uno.*

As I settled into a lounge chair, I spotted the older woman who got an eyeful of Jayson with a Y's ass and pulled my sun hat down over my eyes. There was no way she would know I was the girl on the other side of that ass, but regardless I had to cover my face, if only so *I* didn't have to look at *her*, knowing what I had done.

I was texting my friend Jackie telling her all about Jayson with a Y and "Get that dick," when Jayson with a Y texted me.

"You let me know if you want to see this again, girl," the text said, along with a photo of him shirtless, wearing headphones, and clearly in the locker room at a gym.

*I can't believe he's working out, I'm exhausted,* I thought as I forwarded the picture to Jackie.

"Wow," Jackie wrote back. "Congratulations on getting that dick."

"Right?! He is hot," I wrote back.

"Are you going to get that dick again tonight?" she asked.

"No way. I can't go through that again."

"You should! You might as well—you're always complaining that you aren't having sex."

"I know, but I can't have sex with him again. It wouldn't be right. Somewhere out there is a twenty-five-year-old girl who would appreciate all of his bad lovemaking lingo. I can't rob her of that joy tonight."

I texted his photo to three of my other girlfriends, polished off my hamburger, and headed back to my room to get ready for my shows.

After my second show that night I went straight back to my room. It was around midnight and I was exhausted. I also didn't want to risk running into Jayson with a Y in the casino. I had no idea if he would be there, but I wasn't taking any chances.

Once safely in my room, I turned on the television, cracked open some wine and Peanut M&M's from the minibar, and crawled into bed. I was so happy. *God, I really do like being alone,* I thought.

Then there was a knock on my door. I assumed it was room service; I hadn't ordered any and I figured they were just at the wrong room, but I was a little hungry and wanting to take a look at what someone else had ordered before I decided to tell them the order wasn't actually mine.

Thank God I peeked out the peephole first, because it was not room service, unless Jayson with a Y had started working for the hotel. I ducked, panicked he might have somehow seen me through the peephole.

"You can see out, he can't see in, stupid," I whispered to myself as I crawled across the floor and into a corner.

Jayson with a Y knocked again, rather persistently. And just as I was about to give in, I heard his weird sex voice through the door asking, "Sarah, baby . . . you in there, girl?"

I rolled my eyes and continued to stuff Peanut M&M's in

my mouth, being careful to chew quietly so as not to alert him that I was hiding in a corner like a refugee.

I swear another ten minutes went by before he gave up and went away. Twenty-seven-year-olds are so persistent. About two minutes later, I received another text from him, with another picture of him shirtless—this time in bed—asking if I wanted company tonight.

It was clearly not taken in a bed in the hotel, so I was able to deduce that he had several shirtless photos of himself on deck for emergency situations. And since *he* didn't know that *I* knew he was pounding on my door moments before he texted me, he was trying to make me think he was at home in bed and just casually texting to see if I was around to get that dick.

This is probably going to sound ridiculous, but I thought it was kind of sweet. He was really making an effort to see me again. I thought about what Jackie said, how I was feeling lonely lately and maybe another round with a hot guy wouldn't be a horrible way to end my weekend in Florida.

Then I thought about him calling me "girl" and about the nice older lady who had to look at his smashed-against-the-glass ass when all she wanted to do was enjoy her chicken Caesar by the pool. And I decided against getting that dick one more time. I did, however, order room service and watch a bad movie on TV . . . and it was glorious.

## Maui-Owie

One of our longest breaks when I was a full-time writer on *Chelsea Lately* was over Christmas and New Year's, which is the trickiest time of year to find someone to take a vacation with you when you're single, for obvious reasons. This is a double problem for me because my birthday is December twenty-ninth, so if I want to take a fun trip for my birthday, I have to ask people to try to squeeze me in between holidays. This pretty much rules out any and all married friends.

I always go home to Arkansas for Christmas to see my family, but after about a week there, I'm all set and want to spend the next week facedown on a pool lounge with a cocktail placed right underneath my face and a long straw bringing the frozen joy into my mouth. Specific, I know.

The year my book tour ended I was even more hell-bent on taking a vacation, and luckily my friend Jen was on board. We looked into flights and ultimately decided on Maui. I'd never been to Hawaii and the last time Jen had been there was on her honeymoon, during which she got violently sick. Now she was divorced and appeared to have a stronger stomach. So Maui it was.

Wanting to do it up, we looked into staying at the Four Seasons, but that was all booked—apparently that's where the rest of the world goes in December. So we settled on a place called the Grand Wailea, because they prided themselves on having an "adults only" pool on site. Neither of us has children, neither of us wants children, neither of us hates children, but both of us loved the idea of not having to share our upcoming pool-lounging time with children all ramped up on guava juice, running around screaming and, God forbid, knocking over one of our many cocktails.

Before this, Jen and I had taken a couple weekend getaways together to Santa Monica, which is about twenty minutes from where we live. It may sound silly to take a mini vacation so close to your own home, but the closest I can get to poolside drink service at my house is drinking wine in the bathtub, which can be very dangerous when you live alone and aren't equipped with a med-alert bracelet. We'd also traveled out of the country together for work, as well as on group vacation trips, but this would be our first time spending more than two days together, alone, a long distance from home. This can be a very dangerous thing to do with a good friend because if it doesn't go well, you have to find a way to let said friend know that you'd rather stick your tongue in a blender than ever again spend more than four hours at a time alone with them.

However, I was not worried about that happening with Jen because I know her very well and we both like to do the same thing on vacation—nothing. Neither of us discussed a snorkeling outing or a hike up a fucking volcano. We both just wanted to relax by the hotel pool, wander down to the beach, and flip through reviews on TripAdvisor to determine where we would have dinner each night. Ours was a match made in heaven.

When we arrived at the Grand Wailea, tipsy from our plane ride, we immediately wanted to check out the grounds. As we wandered around, we were both a little overwhelmed by how much of a "family" hotel it was. I mean, we knew that they had a kid-friendly pool to offset the adults-only pool, but I don't think either of us realized that the kid-friendly pool was going to be a mini Disneyland. There were water slides and caves and big round plastic balls that kids could get inside—for what reason, I don't know. I assumed it was so you couldn't hear their screams, but it turned out that when they climbed inside of those plastic balls their screams were pretty much all you could hear.

"Thank God they have a separate pool for us," Jen noted.

"Seriously!" I laughed. "This pool is a disaster."

"Let's go check out *our* pool area," Jen suggested.

"It's probably pretty far away so that you don't even hear the noise from this area," I screamed.

"You don't have to scream. I mean, it is loud here but also I'm standing right next to you."

"Oh, sorry," I said, still screaming.

A waitress walked by and I stopped her to ask how to get to the adult pool.

"Um, just follow the arrows on the wooden signs," she said in a bitchy tone.

"Oh, I didn't see those," I responded defensively.

"They're everywhere," she replied, even bitchier.

"Well, how about you just point to where we should go since you're already standing here and it's taken longer for you to tell us that there are signs we can follow than it would for you to just tell us where the pool is," I shot back, with a huge smile on my face.

The waitress flopped her wrist in a general direction and stomped away, leaving Jen and me alone to diagnose her attitude.

"She's probably hungover," I offered.

"She's probably in a bad mood because she has to work at the kids' pool," Jen retorted.

I decided Jen was correct, then we searched for the wooden sign to point us in the right direction because we assumed Angry Waitress was probably trying to send us to the wrong place on purpose (that may sound paranoid, but we were right).

The adults-only pool was just a few feet away from the kid-friendly pool, which at first had us concerned, but somehow the layout made it seem very serene. I mean, I could still hear the screams of the children running through the pool in plastic balls like panicked hamsters, but it was very, very faint.

We located two cushy lounge chairs and settled in for an afternoon of quietish comfort by the pool. We were immediately greeted by a waiter, who happily took our order and, minutes later, returned with two margaritas. Things were sailing along smoothly, with Jen and I flipping through *Us Weekly*, drinking and tweeting flattering photos of each other. I was just about to doze off when I heard a shrill sound coming from the throat of a girl who was clearly not yet eighteen, even though her squeal was definitely coming from inside the adults-only pool.

I shot up out of my lounge chair, only to see that Jen had already spotted the underage offender. "There, she's right there." Jen pointed.

I slid my sunglasses down my nose so I could get a good look at her, confirming that she was definitely not of age.

"She's like twelve," I noted, irritated.

"She's not even a teenager yet," Jen replied, "that's for sure."

"What the fuck is she doing over here? This is the adults-only pool!" I complained.

Just then we noticed that the tween interloper was not alone—the nonadult also had a few friends with her, *all* of whom were nonadults. We were being invaded!

"We need to do something about this," Jen said in a determined voice.

As if on cue, a security guard passed by. Jen cleared her throat and summoned him over.

"Excuse me," Jen said in her sweetest voice. "Do you see that girl over there?"

The security guard looked over to where we were both pointing. "Yes. What about her?"

"Well, she's like twelve," Jen explained. "And this is the adults-only pool."

I nodded in agreement, unable to speak, due to the straw dangling from my mouth.

"Oh, right." The security guard nodded. "I'll take care of it," he said as he walked away.

Jen and I watched in anticipation as he approached the girl and her friends, ready to see the preteen perps get bounced. But instead all we saw was the security guard walk in their general direction and then veer off to the right without saying a word to them.

"What the fuck was that?" I asked in astonishment as my straw came flying out of my mouth.

"I don't know!"

A few minutes later, the security guard came passing by again and Jen stopped him, this time with a little less sweetness in her voice. "So did you ask those girls to leave the adults-only pool?"

"I did," he lied.

"Oh, well that's weird, because they're still here," Jen said.

"Huh," he said in fake astonishment. "I'll go talk to them again."

Jen and I watched him like hawks as he meandered slowly in their direction. This time he did make it all the way to them, appeared to say something, then quickly walked away. We stared at the group of kids, waiting for them to run off to their designated pool area and respect the segregation that was so clearly noted by the hotel. Instead, they stayed put. They even started laughing loudly, as if whatever the security guard had said to them only made them more comfortable.

When the security guard passed by us again, he moved at a much quicker pace, clearly hoping to bypass us. No such luck, though: we were now on a mission.

"Excuse me!" Jen yelled, her voice now filled with such a strong mixture of sweet and sour it belonged on a Chinese food menu. "Security!? Hi. I couldn't help but notice that those underage kids are still here."

"Yes," the security guard sighed. "They are. I asked them to leave, there isn't much else I can do."

"Oh? Okay," Jen said in what appeared to be a relenting voice. But just as the security guard started to walk away, believing he was now off the hook with the two crazy ladies who wanted the kids to get the fuck out of their pool, Jen followed up with, "I mean, it's your rule, not mine."

The security guard stopped in his tracks, turning to look back at us, a blank look on his face.

"That's right," Jen continued, driving the knife in further. "It's your rule they're breaking, not mine."

The security guard turned and walked away, and I proudly high-fived Jen: "Your rule, not mine," I repeated, using my best Jen Kirkman impression. "You're a genius."

Jen laughed proudly, then noted it was weird that we'd just high-fived, and we both went back to reading our magazines.

Now, if you think that at some point the security guard stepped up and those kids were asked to leave, you're wrong. We spent the rest of the afternoon tweeting the Grand Wailea (@GrandWailea in case you want to have your voice heard), calling the concierge, and just in general talking loudly about the parents of the kids who seemed to think it was cool to let their children shit all over our quiet adult pool time. There was never really a resolution to it, but halfway through the afternoon we went from flat-out annoyed to amused-annoyed and acknowledged to ourselves that we had become slightly obsessed with the situation. This day also happened to be my birthday, so eventually Jen and I left the lies of the adults-only pool behind to take "spontaneous" photos of each other frolicking in the ocean before heading to dinner at Maui's famous Mama's Fish House.

Mama's Fish House was exactly what we were told it would be: a beautiful restaurant with a great view and wonderful food. We enjoyed amazing service and drank our weight in alcohol as we rang in my thirty-eighth year of life. Jen ordered me some sort of chocolate dessert thing that they brought to the table with a single candle in it. When we left, we noticed a canoe on the sand right in front of the restaurant that was just begging for photo ops. So, obviously, we took turns posing in the canoe in varying positions so that we would both return home with hot new "just sitting in a canoe in the moonlight" photos that we could upload to Facebook.

(This trip took place just before Instagram became a thing—you know, back in the days when you had to work even harder to get the pose exactly right because there weren't fifteen filter options for you to choose from in case something on your body was amiss. Jesus, social media makes being single so much more difficult. I never thought I'd miss Polaroids.)

We spent the next two days doing much of the same thing: lying by the pool, rolling our eyes at anyone who was clearly under the appropriate age to be by said pool, and sipping margaritas. There isn't much of a nightlife in Maui; it all closes down very early for the most part, since it's mostly couples who go there. But Jen and I didn't let that get us down. One morning we ordered room service, which came while I was in the shower. When I got out, stoked to see pancakes, Jen was all ramped up about the person who brought our breakfast.

"They asked me if I was Ms. Colonna," she said, annoyed.

"Oh, they thought you were me? That's because the room is in my name."

"I know *that*, but when I said I wasn't you they were like, 'Oh, sorry, wrong room,' and I said, 'No, this is the right room, I'm Ms. Kirkman, Ms. Colonna is just in the shower.'"

"Okay . . . ?"

"And then he looked at the one bed and was like, 'I don't understand,' as if we are the first two women to share a hotel together in Maui."

"I hate that! I hate that people think just because we share a bed we're lesbians. I mean, look at Lucy and Ricky! They had separate twin beds and they were fucking!"

"I'm not sure that's helpful in this argument," Jen noted rationally.

"Oh, right, well you know what I meant."

"I don't but I do," Jen said, confused but in solidarity.

"Anyway it's just annoying that we can't travel together and share a nice king bed without people assuming we're lesbians. Plus, isn't gay marriage legal here, so technically shouldn't they just support us either way?"

"I don't think it's legal here yet but we can definitely come back when it is and see if we're treated with more respect," Jen offered.

Look, I understand that when a man sees two women in a hotel room sharing a king bed he wants to assume it's because they're going down on each other every night. But the reality—and I'm sorry to break the fantasy, guys—is that female platonic friends are comfortable sharing a king bed and usually prefer it because most hotel double beds are about as comfortable as a jail cot.

New Year's Eve, Jen and I walked around fighting the gay rumors that we were sure were floating around about us (in reality, nobody was talking about us at all, gay or straight) and trying to plan what we would do that evening. After asking around, we determined that the place to be for dinner that night was the Four Seasons restaurant, which was within walking distance of our hotel and had an amazing view of the ocean.

"How romantic!" I laughed.

"Exactly, lover!" Jen laughed back as we looked around the adults-only pool for people who were pointing and whispering about us but only spotted a new crop of twelve-year-olds.

"Seriously, this place has a real problem with order," Jen noted.

At around noon, I decided I'd better call the Four Seasons to reserve a table for our nonlesbian New Year's Eve celebration. As you can imagine, since New Year's was that night, they were all booked.

"Oh, no," I said as I hung up the phone, "they're full. They said we can't even get a seat at the bar, it's going to be so busy."

"Call that sushi place the concierge told us about," Jen suggested, "that's fine with me."

I called them, along with about ten other restaurants, only to get the same answer.

"Everything is booked," I sighed, defeated.

Jen looked up from her computer, where she was drafting a complaint e-mail to the guest services division of the Grand Wailea about their horrible lack of rule enforcement at the adult pool. "What are we going to do? I guess we can just eat here?"

Later that evening, we got all gussied up, both of us silently doing our best to not look like lesbians (it was New Year's Eve, after all), and headed down to the restaurant at the Grand Wailea, where we were told we would be given preferential treatment for dinner seating since we were staying there. When we walked in, we were blindsided by the amount of children in the restaurant. Again, I don't have a beef with children, so don't get all pissy with me here, but guess what? Two single ladies on the town on New Year's Eve aren't looking to spend it with families of six. Should two single ladies know better than to vacation in Maui during what is clearly a family holiday? Maybe. But that page on TripAdvisor never popped up and now we were there and we wanted to get hammered without the possibility of a baby seeing it all go down.

"Come on," I said, determined.

"Where are we going?" Jen asked.

"Just follow me."

We walked the pathway to the Four Seasons. When we arrived, it was like arriving at the gates of heaven. It was quiet, serene; the only real noise I heard was waves crashing and glasses clinking together to toast the New Year.

"But we don't have a reservation," Jen exclaimed as I headed up the walkway in my wedges, almost twisting my ankle at every turn.

"*Shhhhhhh.* Just follow me."

When we approached the entrance, there was a man standing there, decked out in a suit and tie, a clipboard in his hand.

"Do you have a reservation?" he asked.

"We do," I lied. "It's under Sarah Colonna."

He studied his clipboard and I looked over my shoulder at Jen, who gave me a "what the fuck" look before I turned back to the gentleman holding the future of our evening in his hands. "Sorry, I don't see it on here," he said, a tone of finality in his voice.

"You don't see it on there?" I asked, incredulous. "I made the reservation weeks ago."

"Spell your name for me again?"

"C-O-L-O-N-N-A," I sighed. "Seriously, I called like three weeks ago. It's New Year's Eve . . . so obviously I called way in advance."

He looked at his clipboard, back at us, back at his clipboard, then back at us for what seemed like twenty minutes but was probably twenty seconds.

"Well?" I asked impatiently as I looked over his shoulder at all the people in the restaurant who were totally our age and who seemed to be having a wonderful time.

"I'm sorry, I don't have your name on here . . . I just don't have a table for you . . ."

My lower lip started to quiver; I'm not sure whether it was on purpose or by accident.

". . . so if you wouldn't mind sitting at the bar for dinner, we can seat you right away. Those seats are supposed to be reserved as well, but clearly this is our mistake," he offered.

"Clearly it is," I said with a smile. "But I appreciate you figuring it out for us."

"I appreciate it, too!" Jen yelled over my shoulder.

"No problem, happy New Year, ladies," he said as he pulled the velvet rope aside and let us into paradise.

"He thinks we're lesbians, too," Jen whispered.

"But we're lesbians with a nice place to eat on New Year's Eve," I noted.

"True. That was really impressive work out there. I can't believe you got us in."

"I know! I feel very proud."

"It's like we got into the adults-only pool when we weren't supposed to!" Jen observed.

"It is! But with steak."

We enjoyed a lovely evening of wine, appetizers, champagne, entrées, and more champagne. We noted that a couple of seats stayed empty all night, so we didn't even feel the guilt of possibly taking someone else's seats with our dirty lies. All in all, it was a successful evening.

When we got back to the Grand Wailea, most people were in bed. There was a fireworks show happening that neither of us gave a shit about, so we decided to go back to our room, order champagne, and ring in the New Year from our hotel balcony. When Jen called to order our cocktails, they immediately asked if she was "Ms. Colonna."

"No, I am her lover," Jen said, deadpan. "A bottle of chilled champagne and two glasses, please."

## Blind-Drunk Date

After I took a pretty long hiatus from dating, one of my friends, Renee, suggested I go out with one of her boyfriend's coworkers. His name was Mike—he and I had actually gone out a couple of times a few years prior, during one of the "breaks" Ryan and I took before moving in together. I kind of wondered, now that I was single, what Mike was up to, but I never bothered to text him or anything, just assuming he had a girlfriend by now. Plus, that whole "recycle" thing hadn't really worked out for me last time. But Mike was cute, had a good job and a nice house, and he liked to cook. I'm reasonably good-looking, have a good job, enjoy nice houses, and love to eat. Why not give this a shot?

Renee suggested that before committing to another date with Mike—she reminded me that the first time we tried to date, he got a little weird about my not having enough free time for him—I should go with her to his birthday party at his house.

"This way, there are a bunch of other people around, including me, so if you aren't feeling interested in him anymore, we can just leave early and you'll save yourself a Friday night down the road," she explained.

"Good call," I agreed. "I forget, how old is he? It's probably like his forty-fi—"

"It's his fiftieth," she interrupted.

"Fiftieth? Oh . . ."

"What, is that too old? I mean, I know he's older than the guys you usually date, but who cares?"

"No, it's not too old," I said, unsure if I meant it. Age doesn't usually matter a ton to me, but fifty just sounded older than I was used to. But then I remembered that I've met a lot of childish fortysomething-year-olds, so maybe the only way to date a man who has his shit together is to date someone with more than a decade on me.

The night of the party, Renee, her boyfriend, and I all went out for pre-party cocktails. By the time we got to the party, Renee was pretty lit up, which is par for the course for her. She's one of those people who likes to "test" strangers when she is out drinking. She has a tendency to go on the attack and if someone is able to spar with her and keep up, she deems them worthy of a conversation. However, if her loud, sometimes offensive antics annoy the person, Renee dubs them an asshole.

When I first met her, I sort of marveled at the way she had the balls to say anything, regardless of who might be insulted. Renee was a tough girl from Brooklyn and I was a not-so-tough girl from Arkansas. But the older we got, the more I realized that the people who were unamused by her weren't the assholes. Not everyone goes to a bar wanting the person next to them to say things like, "So do you like to take it in the ass?" before they even ask you your name.

But Renee had been a friend for a long time and I had a hard time figuring out how to tell her when she was embarrassing me. The few times I tried, she got very angry and defensive, asking me why I was so concerned what other people think.

"I'm not," I told her, "I just think there's a line between trying to start up conversation at a bar and attacking people for no reason."

That led to her not talking to me for a few days, then one day calling me to tell me she wasn't mad at me anymore. I'm not sure what kind of apology that was, but I accepted it. Like I said, we'd been friends for a really long time. I knew her well and I knew that she was a good person. I decided to forget trying to get her to stop acting that way when we went out, and to just start going out with her less.

Anyway, we showed up to Mike's house about an hour after the party started, which I feel is the perfect time to show up at a party when you don't know too many people there. That way, you aren't one of the first few guests standing around like an asshole making awkward small talk with people you barely know, but you're also not there so late that everyone is hammered. Mike looked cute and paid just the right amount of attention to me so that I knew he was glad I was there, but also played polite host to the rest of his guests. At one point, he was talking to Renee and me, and out of nowhere she started talking about how many sexual partners I'd had.

"Just take a guess!" She clapped joyfully.

"Um, no, don't take a guess. . . ," I interrupted, wondering what the fuck she was thinking.

"Oh, don't be a party pooper!" she snapped.

"I don't really need to know—" Mike started to respond.

"But just *guess!*" she said insistently. Luckily, Mike was smart enough to act like he needed to fill a bowl of spinach dip that had clearly just been filled and excused himself.

"What are you doing?" I asked Renee, humiliated.

"What? I'm just having fun," she said nonchalantly.

"This isn't fun, Renee. Seriously, are you wasted or what?"

"Oh, like you've never been drunk before?"

"What?"

"Look, your last boyfriend wasn't comfortable with you and your past. And that was awful. So I think you should make sure the next guy you go out with likes you for who you are."

I actually believe that Renee thought she was coming from a good place when she did things like this (it's possible I believe this too often about people). And she was right; my ex-boyfriend hadn't accepted me for who I was. But I got out of that relationship and vowed never to be with someone like that again.

When I was in my twenties, I was a little bit slutty, that's true. In my defense, I grew up in a small town, so when I moved to Los Angeles I was just excited to have so many options. I mean, I could have sex with people I didn't go to high school with? Jackpot! And if anyone I date wants to have a conversation with me about it, they're welcome to, but it certainly doesn't need to take place at a party with a friend mediating.

Plus, there are some things you grow up and grow out of, and at a certain point in your life you realize what those things are. Yes, I like to drink and have a good time, but things that were funny when I was in my twenties, like falling asleep at bars, lost their charm when I hit my thirties.

I'm not pretending that in my thirties I haven't had some evenings that could technically keep me out of heaven if God is a real stickler for *everything* in the Bible, but the older I've gotten, I've had many, many fewer of those nights.

I knew that arguing with Renee when she had convinced herself that she was being helpful was useless, so I changed the subject and cut the evening short in order to avoid an argument.

The next day, Mike texted me and asked me out on a date for the following weekend.

*Well, Renee didn't scare him off, so if nothing else, he's a durable man,* I thought.

Our date plan was that he would pick me up after a friend's three-year-old's birthday party (I appreciated that he didn't try to get me to attend that event with him) and we would meet Renee and her boyfriend, John, for an early dinner. Hanging out with Renee again might seem like it was a bad idea, but she and I had since talked and I felt like I at least got her to understand that bringing up my sex life was pretty fucking rude, in any situation, but *especially* when I'm with a date.

So around four in the afternoon, Mike knocked on my door. When I opened the door, I could tell that he was either really drunk or had just had a lobotomy. I hoped for the latter.

"Are you okay?" I asked as I watched him sway from side to side, grinning.

"Yeah, I'm great. You ready to go?" He grinned as he twirled his keys in his hand.

"You *drove* here?"

"Duh, yeah. Why?"

"Well, you seem like you've had a few drinks," I said, stating the obvious.

"Well, yeah, I mean how else can you have fun at a kid's birthday party?"

That's when I realized that not only had he shown up to my house hammered, he'd *driven* to my house hammered after attending a child's birthday party.

"Okay, well, I'm not getting in the car with you, so there's that," I said flatly.

"I'm fiiiiine," he slurred.

*Famous last words of a fool.*

"Hang on," I said, shutting the door in his face so I could call Renee and ask her what I should do.

"Just take a cab here to meet us," she suggested. "We're at the restaurant now."

"Well, obviously we're taking a cab, but I don't know if I should even go. I mean, what could possibly go right if this is how it's starting off?"

"Probably nothing, but it will be a really funny story for you to tell later."

She had a point. I mean, I do love a good story . . . and now I'm telling it.

I opened the door and explained to Mike, who was now sweating in addition to swaying, that I would go with him to the restaurant only if we took a cab and if when we got there he drank nothing but water.

"Whatever, fine," he said, his defenses dwindling in the sun.

When we got to the restaurant, Renee and John were prepped and ready for Mike's condition. He did seem to start to get his shit together in the cab, at least briefly, so I hoped maybe the night wouldn't be a total waste. And if nothing else, it would be an early night and I could check hanging out with Renee off my list. A part of me felt guilty that I'd been spending less time with her—probably the same part that had been listening to her give me a hard time about spending less time with her.

She was on her best behavior that night, or maybe it just seemed that way in comparison to the fact that I was on a date with a guy who showed up drunk from a three-year-old's birthday party. It's amazing how comparison can make someone look good by default.

Mike didn't stick to the "water only" rule, and within the hour he started going downhill quickly. Renee and John made fun of him to his face, asking him what kind of game plan it was to show up to a girl's house that way, but Mike wasn't smart or sober enough to pick up on anything that was going on, so for the most part he just giggled when anyone spoke to him.

*Maybe he did have a lobotomy today,* I thought as I watched him try—and fail—to outsmart a ketchup bottle.

After almost an hour and a half, I'd had enough. I was thirty minutes from my house with a guy whom I was definitely never going to speak to again and I had an episode of *True Blood* at home on my DVR that was calling my name. I thought about just grabbing a taxi and leaving him there, but then I felt bad that Renee and John would be stuck trying to figure out what to do with him, even though technically this was all their idea and fault. So, I bit the bullet and told him that he could share a cab to my house, then that cab would continue on to his house. That way I knew my fifty-year-old date would get home safely. Now I know how most of the guys I went out with in my twenties felt—well done, karma.

When we pulled up to my house, I opened the car door on my side, and Mike attempted—and failed—to do the same on his.

"What are you doing?" I asked.

"I'm coming in, aren't I?"

"What? No. You're going home."

"Why?" he asked angrily.

"Because you're wasted and I'm not in the mood to talk to you anymore, or probably ever again."

"What the fuck? Why are you being such a bitch?"

I heard the taxi driver either gasp or stifle a laugh.

"Excuse me? I'm being a bitch? I was being nice by sharing a cab with you so that I could make sure he had your address and that you were awake for at least this much of the ride. I'm getting out now."

"Well, let me walk you to the door to make sure you get in safely," he slurred as he continued to wrestle with the door handle.

"What exactly are you going to do if someone attacks me? Annoy them to death?"

With that I exited the car, then asked the taxi driver if he had the address and apologized to him.

"Well, how am I going to get my car tomorrow?" Mike asked, desperate for a way into my house.

"You're a grown man, I think you can figure it out."

"Fine. Did you pay for this taxi? You need to pay for this taxi."

"I need to pay for this taxi?" I said, my voice rising. "Are you insane?"

"Yeah, I didn't count on paying for a taxi and you're the one who insisted we take one."

"Well, consider it a huge discount from a DUI. You're welcome," I said as I slammed the door. I handed the driver a twenty for a tip, because I felt really bad that he had to spend the next fifteen minutes with that guy.

"That's for you, make sure he pays the full fare for this ride," I whispered.

"Oh, he will. Thank you. But don't worry, I deal with this bullshit all the time," he said as he sped away.

I watched him drive off, and my heart went out to him and every other taxi driver in the world.

After that incident, I started spending even less time with Renee. Similar to my feelings about dating guys like Mike and Patrick, who were prone to little bouts of belligerence when sauced, the last thing I wanted was to spend one of my precious evenings off with Renee in a blackout yelling at me over my taste in television shows—and yes, that actually happened.

**O**ne afternoon, Renee called me and left a really nice message that basically said, "I know you're busy and I know you're never in town, but we can at least catch up on the phone." Now, we all know how I feel about phone calls, but at this point I did have a one-hour daily commute to work at *Chelsea Lately* during which I either listened to Howard Stern or made obligatory phone calls (hands free, of course) to my mom and such. So the next morning, I decided to call Renee on my drive in to work, knowing she would be up getting ready for work, too. This also happened to be right around the time I found out that Alex was married, and to be honest, I knew I could use a friend to talk to about it. Despite her negative qualities, Renee could be a pretty good listener and advice-giver at times. Plus, she'd left such a nice message—maybe our friendship deserved another shot.

"Hi!" Renee answered. "It's eight o'clock in the morning, what are you doing up?"

"I'm driving to work, silly," I laughed.

"Oh, that's right, you call *that* work," she said.

*Ugh, is this really how we're starting off this phone call? With her taking a jab at me?* I wondered.

"Yes. Anyway, how are you?" I asked, changing the subject.

"I'm fiiiiine," she said, slightly slurring.

"Have you been drinking?" I asked.

"Huh? I had a little champagne this morning. What, like you've never drank before?" She scoffed. (This was always her go-to defense.)

"Well, not before work in the morning, no."

"Ohhhhh, good for you," she replied snarkily.

*What the fuck?*

"All right, well—"

"I had one glass, I'm fine."

"All right, well, you sound—"

"Forget it, what's going on with you? I miss you!" she said, her tune changing completely.

"Not much, I've just been out of town a bunch, you know."

"I know! What about boys? Have you met any boys?"

"Um, well. Ugh, yes. I was talking to this guy, his name is Alex . . ."

"Okay, and . . . ?"

"And I don't know. I really liked him and then . . . well, I just figured out that he's married."

Renee started laughing uncontrollably.

"Um, Renee? I'm not joking."

"I know," she said, still laughing.

"Okay, well, I really thought I liked him and, you know, it sucks."

Renee was still laughing, so I just hung up the phone.

A few days later, Renee texted asking me if I wanted to get dinner; I didn't respond. A couple days after that, she called me but I didn't pick up. About a week later, she texted to ask me why I was ignoring her and to say that surely I wasn't too busy to text her back. I didn't respond. The next day, she called me and I decided to pick up.

"Finally! I was beginning to think you were ignoring me," she said before I could even speak.

"Well, I kind of was."

"Why?"

"Because of our phone call the other morning, Renee. That wasn't funny."

"What phone call? What are you talking about?" she asked.

"Are you joking?"

"No, what?!"

"You don't remember me calling you the other morning?"

"I don't know, I get a lot of phone calls—just tell me what you're talking about," she demanded.

That's when I realized she really didn't remember. Or at least she was pretending not to—either way, this was a problem. So I took a deep breath and told her about how I had called her to talk to her about my life, at her request, and when I'd opened up about something that was really bothering me, she had laughed hysterically.

"I'm so sorry. I really don't remember that at all. John and I had a fight and I was drinking a lot the night before, so I think I was still drunk or something and one drink set me off. Please don't be mad at me."

Can you be mad at someone for something they don't remember? I don't know for sure. What I do know is that as much alcohol as I've had in my life, I've never been cruel to someone I love for no reason when drinking, or started fights with complete strangers because I was overserved. I'm not saying I'm the world's greatest drinker—as I said, I've made my share of mistakes—but I'm a pretty harmless one. Unless you count drunken text messages.

I'm not sure if I was mad at Renee or just hurt. Either way, here she was apologizing and I decided the least I could do was accept it. So, we made plans to have dinner a couple nights later. She told me to pick the place and she'd come to me—in a taxi. I mentioned maybe I'd invite another friend of ours, Jess, whom I hadn't seen in a while, and everything seemed good to go. But as usual, it was not.

The afternoon of our dinner date, Renee called me to find out what time she should come over.

"I made a reservation for eight o'clock at that new place by my house. Jess will be here at seven thirty if you want to come by—we can have a drink here first," I told her.

"What? I thought we were staying at your house and ordering in!" she whined.

"Why did you think that?"

"Because that's what we talked about."

"No, it isn't at all what we talked about. I said I'd pick a restaurant."

"Well, I don't feel like going out. I just want to hang out in my pajamas at your house and talk and watch TV."

"Okay, well that's a totally different plan. And Jess already has a babysitter; I doubt she wants to go sit in someone else's house when she has the opportunity to go out."

"Well, what about what I want to do?" she demanded.

"Look, you said, 'Let's go out.' I said I'd make a plan and I did. And quite frankly, I never get the opportunity to go out in this city anymore and I'd like to. So just be here at seven thirty."

"That is not what I want to do. Fine, you and Jess just go out to dinner. I wanted to see you and I can't believe you pulled this!"

"*Pulled what?!*" I yelled. "You said you wanted to go out to dinner and I agreed and now you're acting like I have somehow fucked you over."

"I just don't feel like going out. I feel gross and I'm tired and I just want to stay in."

"Well, that would've been fine a few hours ago, but this last-minute, forget it. You aren't even making sense. This is the most irrational argument I've ever had, and I've had a lot of irrational arguments. You're mad at me for keeping plans with you, basically."

"You guys have fun," she said as she hung up on me.

Look, I understand not feeling like going out—we all go through it, especially girls. One day you just wake up and nothing fits and you hate your life; believe me, I get it. Had this been the only moment of Renee acting like an asshole, I probably would have called Jess, told her to bring her PJs, and ordered a ton of Chinese food. But once again, Renee was lashing out, and I was tired of asking, "How high?" when she told me to jump. I was just done. That was the last time I spoke to her.

Now, before you decide I should have run some kind of intervention for her, she is a grown woman. She lives with her boyfriend. She's quit drinking in the past and I can't say that she acted much differently sober. There is a trigger in her that I don't know how to deal with. We were good friends for well over a decade, and not all of it was terrible. We had some great times together and there were times she was there for me when nobody else was.

But I guess just like relationships, friends can outgrow each other. It's similar to couples who get married in high school—Renee was like my jock high school boyfriend, and it was time for me to move on.

## Parental Misguidance

Probably one of the toughest parts of your parents' getting older is that they lose their parents. Thus, one of the toughest parts of your getting older is watching your parents lose their parents.

At this point, both of my birth parents have lost both of their parents (I clarify "birth" because I have stepparents as well). They both lost their moms before their dads—which I think is a little rude on the men's side. I mean, have some manners and go first, you know? It's called *chivalry*. And because my mom's mom passed away young, at sixty-six years old from cancer, my mom is convinced she knows her own fate.

"I've got two years left," she said to me shortly after her sixty-fourth birthday.

"Mom, don't say that," I replied.

"Well, my mom died at sixty-six and her mom died at sixty-seven."

"So technically you could have three years left," I said sarcastically.

"I guess," she answered. "But cancer got both of them and it's going to get me, too."

"What? Why would you say that?" I yelled, even though I knew why she would say it: she's a fatalist. She constantly worries about everyone and everything. Like when I called her to tell her that I had to have my cat murdered.

"Oh, no. I'm so sorry, poor little guy," she said sympathetically.

"I know! I feel terrible! But he's so sick . . . ," I told her, sobbing.

"Well that's what happens when they get older," she told me. "Elektra is almost nineteen years old," she went on, referring to her own cat. "I don't know how much longer she's going to live, probably not much."

"Well, she seemed okay last time I was home . . ."

"I know, but she doesn't eat much and she's so skinny. I'm sure at some point soon she's going to die," my mom said, starting to cry.

"Mom, don't cry! Elektra is fine. Who knows—she could live for a couple more years!"

"I hope so but I don't think she will," she said, crying harder. "I just don't know what I'll do without her," she sobbed.

"Mom, you can't think that way," I said, finding myself consoling my mom about her healthy cat even though I had called to talk to her about my dying one.

Don't get me wrong: my mother is one of the most caring, wonderful women you'll ever meet. In a situation like this, she isn't trying to turn the conversation around—it's just the way her mind works. It isn't her fault, really. She's worked in a funeral home for almost thirty years—she's surrounded by death on a daily basis, so to her it's just a part of life. I mean, I guess technically death is a part of life for all of us, but to her it's part of her *daily* life.

It can also be very entertaining at times. Like last Mother's Day when I sent a dozen yellow roses to her at work.

"I was so surprised!" she gushed as she called me to tell me they'd arrived.

"Oh, good! I'm glad," I said, very proud of myself.

"Yeah, because when the delivery guy walked in with them I assumed they were for a dead person."

"Well, they were for you. I know they're your favorite," I said, hoping to turn the conversation off of death.

"They are! I told Eric"—Eric is my stepdad—"that when I die I want a yellow-roses casket spray."

"Okay. So, what are you guys doing for—"

"And I want 'Play It Again' by Luke Bryan played at my funeral."

"Noted."

"That's just me. I really do like some religious songs, but I want something more upbeat. Eric says he doesn't mind if it's Luke Bryan as long as it isn't 'That's My Kind of Night,' because that's not really an appropriate song for a funeral."

"Why are you so convinced you're going to go before him?" I asked.

"Well, because . . . your grandma—"

"Never mind!" I interrupted, not wanting to talk about my mom's future death on Mother's Day. Plus, I know she's wrong. She's going to live a long and healthy life, while constantly reminding everyone that she's about to drop dead.

My father lost his mother when I was still in high school, but he lost his dad in the fall of 2012—my grandfather was eighty-eight years old. I remember very distinctly how my sister and I felt when we lost our paternal grandmother, but I wasn't close enough to my dad at the time to really know how it affected him. Obviously, it was hard, but I wasn't there to witness it the way I was when he lost his father because back then we didn't live in the same state.

Since I moved to California, my relationship with my dad has really changed, because we've both really changed. Before, there was some of the usual divorce stuff, where I was mad at him for not being around more, and he wasn't sure how to be around more when we lived 1,546 miles from each other (I just Googled that). Now that we've both matured, we've grown to appreciate each other. Look, that shit takes a while. But, in my opinion, it's like this: I have a great family. Maybe everyone's role hasn't been played out in the "traditional" way, but I wouldn't trade any of them for anything (most of the time).

So at one point, sometime in my mid-twenties, I realized that although my dad may not have been completely present at every point I wished he had been when I was growing up, he wanted to be now—and I could choose to hold on to my crap or I could choose to let it go and have a real relationship with him. So, I chose the latter—and I'm really glad I did because it means a lot to me. He even sat me down one night and told me how much he respected my stepdad for being so wonderful to my sister and me. That took real strength and confidence. He wasn't competing for my love; he was letting me know that he's glad I had a fantastic male role model in my life when he couldn't always be around. I didn't have the heart to then tell him that even though he was correct about my stepdad, most therapists would probably still blame him for some of my poor choices in life.

But to be honest, I think it worked out exactly how it was supposed to. Because now, as an adult, after making the decision to pursue a career that required me to move far away from the family I was around my whole life, I'm lucky enough to still have family within just a couple hours' driving distance from me. I have my dad, my stepmom, her daughter, and my stepniece. They're all pretty amazing. And hey—you can't spell "stepfamily" without "family." (If that phrase takes off at all, I totally coined it.)

When my dad lost his father, it really revealed a lot about my own father to me. He and his dad weren't necessarily that close, but there was a lot of love there. It reminded me a little bit of what our relationship had been like a few years prior, leading me to appreciate my dad even more. I watched him really step up when his dad was sick. Maybe that sounds silly, but it can be easy to just keep looking the other way when things get difficult, especially if you're not much of a constant in one another's lives.

But when my grandpa passed, my dad stepped right up. I was performing in San Diego when it happened, and I'll never forget this moment—because it was kind of ridiculous. My best friend since college, Michele, was living there at the time, and we were just walking out to get ourselves a relaxing manicure-pedicure. I saw that my dad was calling, which I sent to voice mail since I was on my way out. Not because I do that to my dad, but because I do that to pretty much everyone. Knowing this about me, my dad left the news of my grandfather's passing in a voice mail. This may sound harsh, but trust me—it was not. My dad knew me well enough to know that I'd rather hear that than some cryptic "Call me" voice mail that might leave me in a panic if for some reason he couldn't answer when I returned the call. In other words: I'm the asshole.

"My grandpa died," I told Michele as soon as I listened to my dad's message.

"Oh my God, I'm so sorry," she said sympathetically.

"It's okay. I just need to call my dad," I told her.

We stood right by the door of the hotel room while I called my dad. My grandpa had been sick for a while, so we knew it was coming, but that doesn't mean it didn't hurt. All I could think was how much I hated hearing the pain in my dad's voice. I knew I was supposed to feel pain, too—and I did—but mostly it was for my dad. I hadn't seen my grandpa in years. He wasn't the best at being close to his family. He had his own life in this retirement community and he was happy. He didn't send cards and he didn't call. I'm not blaming him for that; after a while I didn't send cards or call either. But my point is, on my dad's side of the family there is definitely a disconnect. That day, however, there was no disconnect in my father's voice—he was hurting.

I asked if he needed me to leave San Diego and he said no. I was working and I'd be back the next day.

"No need for you to cancel a show tonight," he assured me. "You can't do anything right now. I'm okay, Shirley is here," he continued, letting me know my stepmom was right by his side.

After we hung up the phone, Michele looked at me. "Are you okay?"

"Yeah, let's go get those manicures."

"Sarah, we don't have to go do that now. We can just stay here . . ."

"Well, I'm going to need my nails done for the funeral, anyway," I irrationally explained.

As we walked to the nail salon, I wondered what was wrong with me. My grandpa was dead and I wasn't crying. When my mom's dad had passed away the year before, I definitely cried right away. But then again, I grew up with him. I saw him every holiday, every birthday—hell, almost every weekend. It wasn't like that with my dad's dad.

So when the little Asian lady at the nail salon told me to pick a color, I burst into tears.

"Oh, no, sorry. I can pick color for you!" she exclaimed.

"No, no. I can pick the color myself," I told her.

"Should we leave?" Michele asked, unsure of how to handle my sudden outburst.

"No, I'm fine."

"I pick color for you, you sit," the little Asian lady said insistently as she guided me into a chair, then shouted something in another language to the other ladies, who immediately began talking among themselves and trying to avoid eye contact with me.

"Sarah, seriously, we can go back to the hotel," Michele reminded me. "I think it's just starting to hit you—"

"It's not hitting me at all, that's the problem," I said through tears.

"Huh?"

"It's not hitting me. I'm crying because I feel guilty for not crying. That's what is happening right now," I sobbed. "I'm a bad person."

"You're not a bad person."

"I didn't cry when my grandpa died. I'm a bad person."

"You're crying right now and you just found out like five minutes ago," Michele said gently. "I think that counts."

"It doesn't count if I'm crying for the wrong reason!"

"And what's the wrong reason?" Michele asked, baffled.

"That I didn't cry!" I yelled—alerting all the little Asian ladies to my apparent nervous breakdown.

"You want shoulder massage? It helps when I have period," one of the ladies offered.

"What? Oh, no, I don't have my—"

"Yes! She does want a massage!" Michele responded. "And I'll pay for it. Do you guys serve alcohol?"

Since the nail salon did not serve alcohol, once we were finished there, we decided to go get a bite and a drink at the hotel bar. Once we sat down, I called my dad again to check in on him.

"I'm okay," he assured me. "I'm just trying to get in touch with Jeff. I don't have his number."

"You don't know your brother's number?" I asked.

"Well, the one I have for him doesn't seem to be working anymore."

*God, this is so depressing,* I thought.

"Well, I'm friends with his kids on Facebook. I can try to get in touch with them," I offered.

"That would be great, thank you," my dad said, exhausted.

I excused myself, leaving Michele alone at the bar to tackle our order of sushi while I attempted to reach out to the cousins I was friends with on Facebook but not in real life. As annoying as Facebook can be, I guess being able to reach someone you otherwise wouldn't be able to can come in handy at times.

"Hey. Can you have your dad call my dad? He needs to talk

to him. I know this is a weird way to get them in contact, but it's important. Thank you," I wrote to one of my uncle Jeff's kids.

"Just wrote your sister, too. Trying to help my dad contact yours. He needs to talk to him. Here's his number. Sorry for the vague message, but if you can pass that along it's a huge help. Thanks," I wrote to another cousin.

I was so busy trying to connect with long-lost family on Facebook that I didn't even realize I was on a sidewalk outside of a hotel, hunched in a corner, crying.

"Sarah?" I heard an unfamiliar voice call out.

I looked up to see two girls standing right in front of me, concerned expressions on their faces.

"Yeah?"

"Um, we are just going to see your show tonight. We're excited . . . are you okay?"

"Huh? Yeah, I'm great," I said, smiling, as if what they were seeing in front of them was totally normal.

"Okay, cool. So, we'll see you tonight," the other girl said, awkwardly trying to either make me feel better or just get the fuck out of there.

"Yeah!" I smiled as I walked back inside the hotel bar.

I immediately sat down next to Michele and started laughing hysterically.

"What's so funny?" she asked, laughing along with me.

I explained the scene outside to her and we both began laughing even harder.

"I can't even imagine what they must be thinking," I said as we ordered another round of drinks, tears of laughter streaming from my eyes. "I must have looked like a crazy person, all bent over, scrolling through Facebook and crying."

"Please, who hasn't scrolled through Facebook and cried?"

My phone rang again; it was my dad letting me know he'd gotten in touch with his brother, and I felt a big wave of relief knowing that I didn't have to resort to randomly tweeting about my grandpa's death in hopes that someone I was related to would see it.

A few hours later, I went and did my show as planned. Once I got onstage, most of the thoughts of the day left me and I was just performing. Afterward, while I signed books, I avoided eye contact with the two girls who had seen me crying and they politely pretended that the earlier event hadn't happened.

Later, Michele and I found ourselves at a bar that had a mechanical bull. We stood at the bar and made fun of all the dumb girls who were embarrassing themselves trying to ride it, until we had enough cocktails in us that we thought it would be a good idea for us to ride it, too.

The next morning we packed up to leave: me to my dad's and her to her house just a few minutes away.

"My ass hurts," I complained as I zipped up my suitcase.

"You landed right on it when you fell off the bull."

"Oh, that's right."

"I'm pretty sure I got video of it if you want to see."

"No, I'm good."

"Do you want to go get breakfast before we take off?"

"No, I should get going."

"Okay."

"Are you sure I'm not a bad person?" I asked her as the valet pulled my car around.

"For not wanting to get breakfast?"

"Because my grandpa died yesterday and I reacted by riding a mechanical bull."

"Well, the mechanical-bull ride was a reaction to alcohol, not death. And for the last time, you're not a bad person. Everyone deals with grief differently."

"I'm pretty sure I'm the only one who deals with it on a mechanical bull."

"Probably. But your grandpa would have been proud of you last night."

"No way! I was only on that bull for like two seconds."

"It was more like one, but that's not what I'm talking about, stupid. I'm talking about how you got onstage and made people laugh even though you were hurting. That's not an easy thing to do. And you were really, really funny."

"Huh." I pondered. "I did feel like it was a really good show. Maybe I'm just funnier when I'm sad. Maybe I should always try to be sad!" I said with a smile.

"That's not . . . sure, try that," Michele laughed.

On my drive to my dad's, I thought about my grandpa. I thought about how I used to see him every time I visited my dad in the summers, but that slowly started to fade into seeing him every other time, then to every few times. There was never a discussion or a reason for it, it just was. Once he moved to the retirement community he and his wife were living in when he passed, everyone involved seemed to have decided it was too far to drive to the other's house. And once I moved to California, I saw him a handful of times, but that was about it, and at that point I'd lived here for fifteen years. I was always the Christmas-card-sending granddaughter, too. And I'd get one back a couple of weeks later. Then after a while, I stopped getting cards back, so I developed a very mature "well, fuck that" attitude and stopped sending them.

But I had some good memories of my grandpa, mostly of his playing the harmonica, which he was really, really good at. He also did a spot-on Donald Duck impression. These were the things that my father and I sat up and talked about that night while we polished off a couple bottles of wine.

The funeral was a few days later, in Sun Valley, California, where he and his wife had been living for the past decade or so.

"Is Jeff coming?" I asked my dad, curious if his brother was going to make it out for the service.

"No, he wants to, but he and his wife and all the kids just moved to Arizona. He just started a job and it would be too hard to get here."

"Oh. And he can't take off work for the funeral?" I asked sadly.

"It doesn't sound like it. I know he really wants to, but I think with just starting and just moving . . ."

"Yeah, makes sense," I said, even though I wasn't sure it did.

In a way, I understood, and in a way, I didn't. But I also knew that I had just spent an afternoon trying to reach that side of my family through social media outlets, so who was I to judge? I didn't know their situation and I shouldn't pretend to.

As I got ready to drive the hour and a half or so out to my grandpa's funeral, I felt really, really single. There aren't a ton of times it truly bothers me that I'm single—just vacations and weddings. You know, times when you just wish you had a date so nobody thinks you're a lesbian when you share a room with your friend and nobody looks at you all sad when you go find your name card and sit down at a table full of couples.

Going on almost five years of being single, I have focused on the "plus" sides. I have learned to brush off the comments of people back home in Arkansas who "can't believe" I "still haven't gotten married!" I've come to terms with the fact that all of the cousins on my mom's side whom I used to babysit are now married and have children, while I run around the country telling dick jokes. It's the life I chose, and whether it sounds like it or not, I'm very, very happy. I'm proud of myself and I know my family is, too. That's what matters the most to me.

But on this day, I added "funerals" to the short list of times I hate being single. I just wanted someone in the car with me to talk to about how I felt about my grandpa's death—someone who wasn't my dad or a distant cousin on Facebook. But I didn't have that person in my life, and I sure wasn't dragging a girlfriend out to a mobile home retirement community on a Sunday afternoon. Imagine the lesbian rumors I would have sparked in those old hen circles.

Mischief wasn't a fan of car rides, but had he still been alive at this point I probably would have resorted to popping him in the passenger's seat just so I felt a presence next to me. That said, I guess it's good that he wasn't around anymore, because showing up to a funeral with a cat would have probably been considered "rock bottom." So, I did what I always do when I have to go to an event without a date: I got a bikini wax.

That's right, I got a bikini wax before my grandpa's funeral. I didn't get one because I thought I was going to get lucky— that would have been creepy. Plus, that's really never why I get one. I get one because it makes me feel better. I think everyone has an image in their head of a woman who has been single for a long time and doesn't have a ton of sex: her legs are hairy, she has one speck of paint left on her big toe from the last pedicure she got before she gave up, and . . . she has a giant bush. She has all these things because who cares? She ain't got no man! She doesn't need to do all that silly maintenance, right? *Wrong*. I do all of that stuff for me; I always have. It makes me feel good. And if I do happen to end up nude with a gentleman, it's a bonus for both of us that I've kept up with my business. I've had mediocre sex before, but in the middle of it, when I looked up to see my nicely painted toes over a pair of shoulders, I still considered it a win.

I arrived in Sun Valley—a place I would not recommend to anyone—freshly waxed, sporting the obligatory black dress and a pair of heels. The service was held in the community recreational room. It was a depressing place, I can't lie.

*Why is everyone here so old?* I thought as I scanned the crowd, looking for my dad.

"Because your grandpa was old," my dad said as he approached me, clearly reading my mind.

I took in the scene: round tables with paper linens on top, deli trays straight out of the grocery store, giant jugs of lemonade and water.

"This is so depressing," I said as I looked at my dad, tears welling up in both our eyes.

"Your grandpa was happy here, Bones," my dad said as he hugged me, calling me by his childhood nickname for me.

I knew he was right and that was all that mattered. Maybe what depressed me more was that other than my dad, stepmom, stepsister, and grandpa's wife, I didn't know any of the people there. I didn't know anything about the last several years of my grandpa's life. But apparently, my grandpa never mentioned me to any of them either, so I called it even in my head and took a seat on a cold folding chair.

My dad had put together some really nice pamphlets with photos and remembrances of my grandpa. There were pictures stuck to cardboard, full of memories of his eighty-eight years of life. When I found some with me in them, I'd stare at them, trying to remember how I felt in each photo. I found a few pictures of us from a cruise we went on when I was in high school, and I knew in those photos that I felt annoyed—because I was in high school and I was on a cruise with my grandparents. So I kept scanning, until I landed on a photo of us at Disneyland.

*God, I hate Disneyland,* I thought. *Why do I look so happy?*

The answer was simple: I used to love Disneyland. When I was young and I'd come out to visit my dad, we'd go to Disneyland and make it a game to stay up as late as possible. My dad would chant, "Twelve o'clock, twelve o'clock!" when he'd see me and my sister start to fade from a full day of riding Space Mountain and eating churros, encouraging us to make it until Disneyland's midnight curfew. I'd go home to Arkansas sporting mouse ears with my name on them, showing pictures to my jealous friends, telling them tales of the Magic Kingdom.

I smiled, satisfied that I had found a happy memory with my grandpa.

"You used to love Disneyland," my dad said as he stood next to me.

"I know. Why did I like it so much?"

"You weren't old enough to know better."

"True," I laughed.

The service turned out to be quite lovely. His friends got up and said nice things and told funny stories. My dad gave a heartfelt speech. For a service in a brightly lit hall in 105 degree weather, it wasn't so bad.

When I got home that night, I had messages from my cousins on Facebook. They all expressed their grief as well as their regret that they weren't able to attend the funeral, and that they didn't know their grandfather better—one of them had never even met him. A few days later, I received a letter (like a real, handwritten one) from my uncle Jeff, also expressing his grief. It was such a beautiful letter; I sat down and wrote him back immediately, probably the first letter I'd written in years.

The one constant in all of the correspondence was that we all agreed it was fucked up that we had this family we didn't even know. Life is precious; family is precious. We shouldn't be taking any of it for granted.

Our communication dropped off again after a few weeks. But I know we all meant it when we said we missed each other. We just have a weird way of showing it.

## Two Hundred Cigarettes

There was a good four-month stretch in the beginning of 2013 when I spent every evening on my balcony, drinking an entire bottle of wine, listening to country music, and smoking a pack of cigarettes. I'm not a smoker and I prefer vodka, so, in what I assume was a depression, I didn't even have the decency to abuse myself with things I really liked. And since, as I've mentioned a few times, I felt my social life was suffering due to my professional life, this also was not a proactive way to spend my time off. However, it was all I wanted to do and all I could bring myself to do.

These smoke-filled nights, I'd turn on my television, keeping the volume down so that it didn't interfere with my country music but would allow some other movement in my house—it gave me the feeling of having other people around without actually having to allow other people around. It was a sad scene, comparable only to what I imagine the prequel of any episode of the Oxygen channel's *Snapped* would look like.

I didn't tell any of my friends what I was doing during those evenings, blowing off fun dinners and whatnot with the excuse that I was just tired. I guess that wasn't really a lie, because smoking a pack of cigarettes and drinking a bottle of wine every night is exhausting. But one night I picked up the phone (me? Calling someone?) and told my friend Liz (a.k.a. "Two Rings") what I'd been up to.

"It's okay, Sarah. You're just depressed. Don't beat yourself up over this," she offered gently.

"Okay, thanks. So it's okay?" I asked tearily.

"Well, no, I mean you have to stop doing it but just don't beat yourself up about it."

"When do I have to stop doing it? It's really kind of nice."

"Is it?"

"No."

"Then stop."

Liz was right: I wasn't enjoying myself, obviously, and I needed to break the pattern. Of course, it took a little while to truly break it. For a few weeks I'd do things like go meet friends for dinner but jet out early so I could get home, smoke a couple of cigarettes, drink a glass of wine and listen to one country song. I was like a sad addict, weaning myself off of my sadness slowly. I just wasn't ready to go cold turkey, plus the chair on my balcony was really comfortable.

- - -

My mom is also a big fan of country music, and like me, of Luke Bryan. But she has what is bordering on an unhealthy obsession with him. At first I thought, *Well, she just really likes him because he's super hot,* because—well, he's super hot. But she straightened me out one day by letting me know that she likes him because he is (a) amazing and (b) really grateful for his success.

"Oh," I told her. "I thought it was because you wanted to do it with him."

"He's much younger than me, Sarah, don't be ridiculous. Plus I love Eric."

"Well that's a relief," I laughed.

"But if I was single . . ."

"Let's just leave it at you love Eric."

One Christmas, I surprised her with tickets to a Luke Bryan concert. She wanted to see him live before she died, and since according to her that could be any minute, I decided to help her check that off the bucket list. I hid the tickets in a country music magazine, which I then wrapped. Christmas morning, I was so excited for her to open that gift, which is unusual for me because usually I'm just focused on counting how many presents I have in my pile in comparison to my sister's pile. Yes, I'm an adult.

When she unwrapped the country magazine, she stared blankly at it for a second and then smiled.

"Oh, cool, you got me a subscription to *Country Weekly*!" she said, genuinely excited.

*Fuck, she seems really happy and that would have been so much cheaper.*

"Well, look inside the magazine, Cheryl!" Eric said impatiently. He wanted to see her face when she realized she had Luke Bryan tickets just as much as I did. Plus, he had a couple of his own presents left to open and she was cutting into his time.

When she finally saw the tickets, she stared at them for a while and appeared to be sweating. For a moment I thought we actually were going to lose her.

"These are tickets to see Luke Bryan," she finally said, slightly emotionless.

"Yes, yes they are." I nodded.

"But I'm not Allen Davis," she said, reading the name that was on the tickets.

"Oh, I know. I got them off of StubHub, that's just who I bought them from."

"But they won't let me in if I'm not Allen Davis, will they?"

Clearly my mother had not yet delved into the world of StubHub, but after a few minutes of gentle explanation, she got it.

"Oh my *GOD I'M GOING TO A LUKE BRYAN CONCERT*!"

"Yes you are!" I laughed.

"*Honeypot, we are going to a Luke Bryan concert!*" she squealed to my stepdad, using their endearing yet nonsensical pet name for each other.

"I know, Cheryl. Sarah told me about it before she bought them because she wanted to make sure we could go. It's in Missouri."

"Missouri . . . in February," she said, her brow furrowing.

"What's wrong, Mom?" I asked.

"Well, what if it snows and we can't go?" she asked, the fatalist rearing her ugly head.

"It's going to be fine, honeypot," my stepdad assured her.

And it was fine. It did snow, but they still successfully made it to Missouri to see Luke Bryan, although on the day of the concert, her coworkers concocted a very official-looking text informing her that the concert was canceled due to weather. They're real jokesters over at that funeral home. But they didn't fool her for long, as she realized that her phone number wouldn't have been attached to the tickets. Allen Davis would have gotten that text, because Allen Davis was the poor fool who gave up his tickets to see Luke Bryan, and she was no Allen Davis.

**A**bout a year later, just around the time I was weaning myself off of sad balcony time, the subject of my mom and I going to see a Luke Bryan concert together in Tulsa came up. I don't get back to Arkansas that often and she and I had never taken a trip to do anything like that by ourselves before, so it sounded like it might be a good idea—except the part about Tulsa.

By this time, Luke (we are on a first-name basis now) had been on *Chelsea Lately*, so I had met him. I came onstage during his interview and "crashed" it, which was a pre-written bit, but he didn't know it was going to happen; however, he was a great sport about it. I also informed him that my mom was his number one fan, to which he responded:

"Well, any time you guys come to a show let us know and we'll do a meet-and-greet."

Now he'd really fucked himself.

I contacted his tour manager and set everything up so that when my mom and I went to his show in Tulsa, she'd get to meet her idol. Then I called her and informed her what was going to happen—no way I was going to surprise her with this one; she needed time to process it all so that when she did meet him she didn't completely humiliate both of us.

"We are going to meet him?" she asked flatly. She was way too calm about this; it was very serial killer–like.

"Yep, it's all set up!"

*"Oh my God, I can't believe it!"* She squealed.

"I know, it's going to be so fun," I told her, relieved she was showing emotion again.

"Okay, so you'll fly here Friday night and we'll drive to Tulsa Saturday morning?"

"Oh, I was thinking I'd fly into Tulsa and just meet you there. I have to go back to L.A. Sunday, so it doesn't make sense for me to fly to Arkansas first, then drive an hour and a half."

"Well, how am I going to get to Tulsa?" she asked.

"Well, I figured you'd drive."

"Well, I don't know how to get there."

"Mom, I used to fly into Tulsa all the time and you guys would pick me up."

"Yeah, but Eric drove, I didn't pay attention how to get there."

"Well, it isn't that hard and your car has GPS."

"I don't want to drive myself to Tulsa! What if something happens?"

"Mom, you drive every day. Why are you talking like you're ninety-seven years old all of a sudden?"

"I drive every day here, not to Tulsa!"

"Mom, it just doesn't make sense. It's all this extra traveling for me and all I do is travel. I just want to go to Tulsa because it's easier."

"Well, maybe Eric can drive me," she offered, not backing down on her inability to locate Tulsa.

"But we only have two tickets."

"He can just hang out in the hotel room while we go to the concert."

I knew that my stepdad would do exactly that if she asked him to, so I sucked it up and said I'd fly home and drive us to Tulsa and back.

"Oh, good!" she said, relieved. "It'll be fun. Road trip!"

"Yeah, road trip . . . to Tulsa."

"Oh, Tulsa is fine. What hotel should we stay in? We should stay in one close to the venue because I bet traffic gets really bad right before and we don't want to be late, could you imagine if we got stuck in traffic and couldn't move and just missed the whole thing . . ." She started reeling, worrying about potential disasters as usual.

"I'll find a hotel close to the venue and I'll book our rooms."

*"Rooms?"* she repeated. "We aren't sharing a room?"

Coming off of my depression, I wasn't sure sharing a hotel room with my mom in Tulsa was the way to go. I mean, I'm an adult! Aren't adults supposed to have their own rooms? But I could hear the disappointment in her voice and knew I was going to have to suck it up again. Plus, if I was sharing a room with my mom I wouldn't be able to come back after the concert and drink and chain-smoke. Without knowing it, she would be kind of like my sober companion.

The day finally arrived and my mom and I headed to Tulsa. We checked into our hotel, my mom excitedly telling the girl at the registration desk that she was going to meet Luke Bryan that night.

"Wow, that's awesome." The girl smiled.

"Yep. My daughter here is on TV and she met Luke one day and told him I'm his biggest fan so he said he wanted to meet me."

The girl looked at me, either trying to place my face or figure out if my mom had Alzheimer's.

"That's exactly how it happened," I said as I took the hotel keys from her hand.

Mom and I got ready; I put on my brand-new cowboy boots that I was uncomfortably excited about and she put on her Luke Bryan T-shirt that was about two sizes too big for her.

"Mom, that shirt is kind of big," I told her as I put on a final coat of mascara.

"It's a men's medium," she explained.

"Well, tonight why don't we get you a woman's T-shirt? One that fits?"

"I don't like those. I'm sixty-three years old, I'm not going to wear a belly shirt."

"They aren't belly shirts, Mom. We'll just get you a large woman's—"

"I don't like those shirts, they're too tight in the tits."

That was the end of that discussion. Mainly because I was shocked to hear my mom say the word "tits."

The whole day, I was terrified that something would go wrong and we wouldn't get to meet Luke Bryan. But minus a couple of instances of being sent to the wrong window to pick up passes, everything went smoothly, and before I knew it my mom and I were backstage, ready to meet Luke. It's possible I was more excited than her.

His tour manager pulled us to the side while the regular

meet-and-greet went on. We weren't there for that bullshit! We were getting one-on-one time. I started sweating. *Seriously? This always happens when good-looking men are around! Must be that early menopause,* I thought as I clenched my armpits.

"Sarah?" I heard the voice of an angel (Luke Bryan) call out. "You got your momma with you?"

I looked at my mom and she looked like she was going to pass out.

"I sure do!" I said in a weird *Beverly Hillbillies*–type tone that I'd never heard come out of my mouth before.

He called us into the room and went right to my mom for a hug, then to me. He talked to us for like twenty minutes, babbling nonstop about his tour, asking me how work was, and taking my mom's advice on which songs from his album should be released first. At one point, he mentioned something about FM radio, and my mom interrupted:

"AM, FM, XM, too . . ." She smiled, quoting his own song lyrics to his face.

I wanted to be embarrassed, but I couldn't be. It was adorable and he loved it. Plus, when I was in my early twenties I met Vince Neil at a restaurant. After politely saying hello, he excused himself to the "little boys' room," to which I responded by excitedly shouting the lyrics to "Smokin' in the Boys Room" right to his face. At least now I knew where I got it.

Luke's tour manager reminded him that he had a show to

do, so we took a photo with him and headed out to our seats. It's slightly annoying that you can't see my cowboy boots in this picture.

The rest of the night was really fun; he put on an amazing show and my mom and I sang our hearts out. We have equally terrible voices.

After the concert, my mom thought maybe I should text the tour manager to see if there was an after-party.

"Did you just say *after-party*?" I asked. First she said "tits," now, "after-party"? It was like the world as I knew it was ending.

"Yeah, we are groupies now, you need to learn the lingo," she explained.

We opted against actually trying to track down an "after-party," mostly because my mom had been so well behaved and I didn't want to watch her go off the deep end. We went back to the hotel and checked to see if the bar was open for a night-cap, but it was closed. So we went back upstairs and got in bed.

"Oh my God, Luke Bryan tweetered about me!" my mom yelled from the double bed next to me.

"What? It's *tweeted*. And . . . you have a Twitter account?"

"Yeah but I don't twat—"

"*TWEET.*"

"Well I don't tweet, I just use it to follow you and Luke. But, look!"

I had tweeted that we had a great time at Luke's show and he wrote back, "Thanks, darlin', your momma is the best."

"*See!* He tweetered about me!"

"He called me *darlin*'," I marveled.

We both went to sleep with big smiles on our faces.

The next morning, I drove my mom back to Arkansas, then boarded a plane home to Los Angeles. As the plane took off, I thought about the previous night. Of all the relationships that I worry have suffered because I haven't been around to put the time into them, it had never occurred to me that my mom might be one of them. But spending time with her like that made me crave more of it, and I made a note to myself to remember the feeling I had that weekend. For the first time in a while, I'd had fun. I'd felt happy.

I walked into my apartment and went right to bed—that night, I didn't need a cigarette or a glass of wine to get me to sleep.

# Reverse Catfishing

To celebrate my upcoming thirty-ninth birthday (which everyone would be out of town for), I went out to dinner with three of my closest girlfriends: Jackie, Tilley, and Erika, the same three girls who came over when I had to have my cat murdered—see, we do fun things together, too! I've known all of them for a very long time, so it's interesting to look around the table at that point in our lives and see how each person's life has changed.

Jackie and I met when we were both bartending. She got married once, on a whim in Mexico, way too quickly, and ended up sleeping on my couch for a while during the divorce—which wasn't really a divorce because their marriage wasn't even legal in the United States. She was always attracted to the kinds of guys who don't make great boyfriends (no car or job or the ability to fill out proper paperwork to get married in Mexico). But she grew out of that and is now with the man who I believe is her soul mate. They even have this whole sappy romantic story about how they dated many years ago and found each other again. It's pretty gross. But it's also pretty great.

Tilley has had a few serious relationships but none that were ever quite the right fit. She came close a couple times, but there was usually something that kept the relationship from being "the one." But she's now married to "the one" and happy as can be. Her husband is truly her partner and best friend in every way. They have great conversations, they have great sex (from what she tells me; I haven't watched or anything), and they even take spin classes together, which I do like to make fun of because I think that couples who work out together are assholes.

And Erika has been single for quite a while but has recently started dating someone she has known for many, many years and is happier than I've seen her in any previous relationship. He also seems very happy and he seems to worship her, which I approve of wholeheartedly.

So, at this table full of close friends, I was the odd one out with no husband, no boyfriend, and no prospect in the wings. I don't mind being the single friend most of the time, I really don't. It only bothers me occasionally, when a voice creeps into my head and says, "What if you just never meet anyone ever again?"

That exact thought ran through my mind as we sat, sipping cocktails, celebrating the final year of my ability to turn an age that begins with the number "three," when the subject of my dating life inevitably came up.

"It's just impossible for me to meet people," I explained to my three friends as if they hadn't heard this speech before. "Seriously. Impossible."

"I don't think it's *impossible*," Tilley replied.

"It is," I said, hoping to put an end to this particular conversation.

"I think you could meet someone if you wanted to," Jackie chimed in.

"Me too," Tilley agreed.

"Where?" I asked, annoyed. "At a comedy club? When I'm working? That's not the way to meet people. It's work."

"Well, you met that one guy in Florida who told you to get his dick," Jackie said.

"Yes. And that little romp scarred me for life. Sometimes when I go to sleep I hear that weird voice in my head saying, 'Get that dick, get that dick,' and I break out into a cold sweat."

"There have to be places where you can meet someone," Tilley said, pressing me.

"Okay, where? On the plane on my way home from a gig? That only happens in movies with Meg Ryan and her previous face."

"I agree with Colonna," Erika interjected. "I was not meeting anyone anywhere. The only reason Derek and I worked out is because we've known each other for years."

"You're both wrong," Tilley said as she sipped her white wine. "I bet you could meet someone if you wanted to. I think you're just closed off to it."

It occurred to me that Jackie said basically the same thing to me in Cabo. But I wasn't about to bring that up. So instead I said: "I'm not closed off to it! I just don't want to date another comic or an audience member or a gay male flight attendant. And for the past three years or so, those are the only people I meet."

"Because you're closed off to it," Jackie threw in.

"Isn't this supposed to be my birthday dinner? Can we change the subject?"

"What about online dating?" Tilley asked.

"Okay, I guess we can't change the subject," I sighed.

"Seriously," Tilley went on, "lots of girls I know at work meet guys online all the time."

"It's too much work. I don't have time to sit on my computer and make fucking pen pals."

"Then let me do it for you," Tilley offered.

"Yeah right," I laughed.

"I'm dead serious."

"You want to go online and pretend to be me? Isn't that 'catfishing'? I've seen that shit on MTV and it never works out well."

"Well, it's not really catfishing because you'd actually show up on the dates. When people catfish they're pretending to be someone that doesn't exist," Erika explained, sort of.

"So it's reverse catfishing," I said.

"I think so," Jackie said. We were all confused.

"Call it whatever you want, just let me do it," Tilley demanded. "For three months, let me run your dating life. I'm going to use online dating sites, talk to matchmakers, find out about social events where you can meet people . . ."

"Wow, it sounds like you've thought about this for a while," I told her. "Which is both sweet and creepy."

"I have thought about it; I just didn't think you'd let me do it."

"Well, I haven't said yes yet," I reminded her.

"It's easy! I'll do everything. You just have to show up on the dates I set up and you have to do what I tell you to do. You have to be open to different things that are out of your comfort zone. For six months, just let me—"

"Wait, a minute ago you said three months!"

"I know, but I'm going to need six months. It's going to be a process," she said. She had switched into Business Tilley, the organized, strategic Tilley who has a huge job in a giant corporation—the Tilley whom none of us see that often.

"Is this what you're like at work?" Jackie asked.

"I guess so," Tilley laughed.

"No wonder you have such a good job. You're scary," I told her.

"So are you in?" she demanded.

"I think you should let The Advisor do this," Erika suggested, referring to Tilley's nickname.

"The Advisor" was a name we came up with for her during a girls' weekend in Palm Springs. Tilley, always very careful to protect her face from the sun, walked out to the pool at the house we were renting wearing one of those giant visors I've only ever seen gardeners and little old Asian ladies wearing. We all made fun of her while she delicately climbed onto a raft and floated around with her face well shaded.

"Whatever, laugh all you want. We'll see who still looks good in twenty years," she said, unfazed by our teasing.

Later that afternoon, we sat by the pool discussing one of the other girls' relationship problems. Tilley got very serious at one point and began breaking down the reasons behind the girl's current issues, and as usual, she was spot-on. By the time she was finished, the girl was on the phone with her boyfriend and they were having a great, honest conversation.

"You're really good at giving advice," Jackie marveled.

"Seriously, you're a really good ad-visor," Erika laughed. "Get it? Ad-*visor*!"

We all thought this was the funniest thing in the world, immediately dismantling Tilley's hard work and insight, going right back to making fun of her hat and suggesting she open up a little booth with a sign that said THE ADVISOR on it.

But I agreed with Erika. If anybody could find the right guy for me, it was The Advisor.

"Okay, fine. I'm in," I promised her. "But only because your neck veins are kind of bulging right now and I'm afraid to say no."

"Ha ha, very funny," she said as she signaled the waiter to bring us another round of drinks. "This is going to be great. You have to do what I say, though. Promise?"

"I promise," I laughed. I actually kind of liked the idea of someone doing all that work for me and just telling me where to be and who I'd be meeting. Plus, what did I have to lose?

"Awesome," Tilley said, pleased. "I'm going to need your credit card information."

"Wait, why?"

"To join a couple of dating websites, dumbass. We aren't going the 'free profile' route—you'll never meet anyone that way."

"Okay. Just don't put me on FarmersOnly or anything weird like that."

"If I was single I would totally be on FarmersOnly," Erika interjected. "I wouldn't mind dating a farmer. You'd always have nice vegetables."

"But you're not a farmer," I explained.

"You have to be a farmer to be on that website?" Erika asked.

"Yeah. That's why it's called FarmersOnly," I explained, "because it's for farmers. *Only.*"

"Ohhhhh, I just thought it was a place you could meet farmers if you wanted to," Erika went on.

"You're thinking of JDate. You don't have to be Jewish to find a Jew on that site; farmers are clearly more exclusive," explained Jackie.

"Don't worry, I won't put you on there. I'm going to research the ones with the best success rates and go from there."

"How'll you have time to do all of this?" I asked.

"I'll do it at night. I'm going to get Thomas"—Thomas is Tilley's husband—"involved. He loves this kind of shit. We'll drink wine and look at guys' profiles for you."

"That sounds romantic," I said.

"It'll be nice bonding time for us."

The night rounded out with the four of us going to our favorite old local spot in Hollywood and getting really drunk. You know, like adults.

A couple of days later, Tilley e-mailed me. "What is the last book you read? And don't ask any questions, just answer."

*Geez, she is really bossy. And I like it.*

"*Home Front* by Kristin Hannah," I wrote back. "I would ask how you're doing but you told me not to ask any questions."

"I forgot to put 'smart-ass' in your 'About Me' section."

About a week later, Tilley called me. Since she's well aware I'm not a phone person, I figured she had news.

"What's up?" I answered.

"Okay, we've got a couple of things brewing here: a couple of guys who seem pretty awesome. One of them is going to text you. I'll send you all of your correspondence with him so far so you know what you guys have talked about."

"This is so weird but also amazing."

"I know. I'll also send you a picture of him now that you've agreed to go out with him. Remember to keep an open mind," she warned me.

"Well, that doesn't sound good."

"That's not what I mean. He's cute, he's just not your typical type, but that's good because your typical type usually turn out to be assholes."

"Ugh, okay. Can you just tell me what you mean by 'cute'?" I asked.

"I just sent you the picture. Look at your e-mail."

"Okay, stay on the phone with me," I said as I walked over to my computer and opened the e-mail.

"Well?" she asked impatiently.

"Hmmmm. I don't know. I mean, I guess he's kind of cute? But he looks like he might be pretty chubby. Is there a full-body photo on his profile?"

"No."

"Exactly. He's hiding something. And that something is his body."

"Well, he might be a little chubby but that's okay. You're branching out. No more athletes. No more guys with six-packs."

"But why?" I whined.

"How many good guys do you know who have six-packs?" Tilley demanded.

"Point taken. But that doesn't mean I have to date someone who's in the 'heart attack danger' weight zone."

"Oh, stop. He doesn't look like he's that big."

"Then why is he hiding his body?"

"Because of people like you who may not give him a chance and meet him in person!"

"Ugh. Fine. I'll meet him. What does he do?"

"I'm not sure what his job is."

"Ugh."

"But he seems really funny and he has a similar sense of humor as you. Just go on one stupid date with him. He's really into live music, too, and I know how much you like going to concerts. And look at his hair! He has a great head of hair."

"Are you sure *you* don't want to go out with him?"

"Be quiet. I have to go, text me when you hear from him," she said before abruptly hanging up the phone. She was either busy or didn't want to risk my talking myself out of the date.

About an hour later, I received a text from live-music-lover guy: "Hi Sarah, it's Philip. Just wanted to touch base with you. Can I call you?"

I immediately texted Tilley. "He wants to call me. What should I say?"

"Say yes," she wrote back immediately.

"But I hate talking on the phone. Why can't he just keep texting me?"

"Because some people think it's rude not to talk on the phone, Colonna. He's trying to be a gentleman. I think that's a good sign."

"I know, but can't I just write back that I hate talking on the phone and we can just text instead?"

"No."

"Why not?"

"Because I told you to say he can call you and you promised to do whatever I tell you to do," she shot back.

"Fine. You're mean," I responded. "But also I love you and thank you for trying to make sure I don't die alone."

"You're welcome."

So I took a deep breath and texted Philip back. "Sure, I'm around now if you wanna talk."

A few seconds later, my phone rang. *Ugh, I have to answer. It would be really weird to tell him I'm free now and not answer. Right?* I asked myself. *Right.*

"Hello?"

"Hi," the voice on the other end said, followed by complete silence.

I waited for him to announce himself or say something else . . . but he didn't.

"Um, is this Philip?" I asked.

"Yes," Philip responded.

More complete silence.

"Okay, great," I said, not sure what the fuck was going on. "What's up?"

"Oh, nothing."

More complete silence.

"Okay, great," I repeated.

More complete silence.

"Philip?"

"Yes?"

"Oh, just making sure you were there. You know. You just weren't talking . . ."

"I'm here."

More complete silence.

"Okay, well, you said you wanted to talk so . . ."

"Yeah. I figured we should talk before we meet this week."

*A whole sentence! Hallelujah!*

"Yeah, great. So, what's up?" I asked again.

"Not much."

Dead silence. The rest of the conversation went exactly this way: with me rummaging up questions and him giving one-word answers. I felt like I was being pranked. Finally, I decided I had to either get off the phone or throw it against a wall.

"So I should get going," I said after having a ten-minute one-sided conversation.

"When do you want to meet?" Philip asked.

"I can meet Wednesday or Thursday," I offered.

"That works. Is ten thirty good?"

"Ten thirty p.m.?" I asked. I knew the answer was yes but it sounded kind of late to meet for a first date. I realize I'm not the most traditional-seeming person in the world, but if I'm trying to actually find someone, we can meet at eight o'clock like normal people. Plus, I've seen *The Craigslist Killer* on Lifetime. I'm no fool. "That's kind of late for me," I told him.

"Well, I go see shows and I'm not done until then."

"Shows?"

"Yeah, live music."

"Oh, then we can do another night if you already have tickets those nights."

"No, I do it every night. I don't have tickets. I just look up local places and pick where I want to go."

"Do you do that for work? Are you like a music agent or something?"

"No."

More silence.

"Okay, so you just go . . . ?"

"Because I like live music. It's my thing. I go seven nights a week unless I'm doing an open mic."

"Ohhhh, you're a musician?" I asked, kind of interested.

"No."

Silence.

"Philip?"

"Yes?"

"What do you do, Philip?" I said, trying not to sound annoyed. *Is this guy on the spectrum or what?*

"Oh. The open mics? I'm a comedian. Well, trying to be, anyway."

*FML.*

"Okay, cool. So I'm not sure about this week since you need to meet so late and I have a long week. Maybe next week or something," I threw out, knowing I was never going to meet him but really wanting to get off the phone.

"Okay."

Silence.

"Okay, bye, Philip," I said as fast as possible, then hung up.

I called Tilley immediately after and told her all about my horrible, dead-end conversation with Philip.

"So basically, he goes and watches live music every night of the week like some sort of annoying hipster, which is not something I'm into and not a sign of someone who is very productive in their daily life," I explained.

"Yeah, that's not great," she admitted.

"Oh, and he's an aspiring comedian. I can't go out with him. I've tried that and it's always a disaster!"

"Okay, I will admit that he doesn't sound like the one or anything, but maybe you should just meet him—"

"No way. Please don't make me! This would never work. He didn't even speak. It was torture! Plus, I can't date an aspiring comedian," I whined.

"Okay, you don't have to go out with him. But you should tell him. I think honesty is good and it'll help you meet the right kind of guy."

"Fair enough. But I can text him, right? I can't go through another conversation like that."

"Yes. Text him."

The next day, Philip texted me to let me know that his Friday night had just opened up so he could also meet at ten thirty that night, if a weekend night was better for me.

*I would never waste a Friday night when I'm actually in town on a first date. Never. Well, maybe for George Clooney.*

I decided to write him back immediately to let him know that we were no longer going on a date and that he should continue his online pursuit of other women. I didn't see the point in wasting his time—I was being considerate of his super-busy live-music barhopping schedule . . .

"Sorry, after we got off the phone I thought about it and I don't think we are a good match. I'm not much into the nightly music scene and I'm actually a comedian as well. I'm hoping to find someone in a different field of work than I'm in. Hope that makes sense."

Seconds later, I received his response: "Okay."

Ah, classic Philip.

Tilley had a couple more guys in the works from whatever website she had signed me up for, but she was determined to explore other options, so at one point she had me on the phone (this was the most I'd talked on the phone in years) with a matchmaking agency. The woman I spoke to seemed very together and very invested in finding the right guy for me. When I told her about my brief experience with Philip, she scoffed at the foibles of online dating and assured me that I wouldn't have to deal with any of that nonsense if I signed on with her. She and her "team" would sit down with me personally and really get to know me and what it is I'm looking for in a partner. And then they would sit down with all of the men they thought would be right for me, filter out the ones who didn't fit my every need, and introduce me to the ones who did. It sounded amazing. The way this lady was talking, I'd be riding off into the sunset with my true love in no time.

"This sounds perfect!" I told her excitedly toward the end of our call. "So what do I do next?"

"Well, you just need to come in and meet with us, fill out some paperwork, pay our annual fee of fifteen thousand dollars, and we will get to work!"

"Um, did you just say fifteen *thousand* dollars?"

"Yes. It might sound steep but if you really are invested in finding—"

"I'm not. Bye!" I said cheerily as I hung up the phone. I wasn't trying to be rude, but I knew if I let her go on too long she'd talk me into it by setting up some sort of payment plan or something because I'd guilt myself into believing that if I really wanted to find someone, this was the only way. As promised, I immediately called Tilley to tell her how that call went.

"Well?" she asked excitedly. "Was she as awesome as she says she is?"

"She seems pretty awesome, yes," I admitted.

"Great. So you're going to do this, right?"

"She charges fifteen thousand dollars."

"Oh, fuck that!" Tilley said, horrified.

I was so relieved. I was kind of afraid Tilley would also

think I needed to "invest in my future," which would involve dipping into my retirement savings . . . but my retirement savings *is* me investing in my future, so that would be like cutting off my nose to spite my vagina.

"Oh my God, I'm so glad you agree! I wasn't sure if you would think I should do it," I admitted.

"Are you insane? I thought it would be like fifteen *hundred* or something. I'll look into other agencies. Can you go to a social mixer at a museum next weekend? I found it on this singles website. I'll go with you."

"That sounds awful," I told her.

"I told you to do what I say. And they're serving wine."

She really knew how to get to me.

"Okay, fine, I'll go."

"Good girl."

"Wait! I have shows in Jacksonville that weekend! I can't go!" I said excitedly. I'd never been so thrilled to be going to Jacksonville—I don't think anybody ever has.

"God, you really are out of town all the time. No wonder you can't meet anybody."

"I can't believe you just admitted that! Finally."

"I'm not admitting shit. I'm just saying your schedule is challenging, but I love a good challenge."

"Clearly," I laughed. *The Advisor doesn't fuck around.*

"Okay, one more thing: I have another guy from online. I—well, you—asked this one what he does for a living so we wouldn't have another comedian situation. He's an editor—

edits commercials or something like that—but it sounds like he works a lot and has his shit together. You're going to meet him for drinks this week."

"Okay, that sounds . . . better," I said cautiously. I was still having a hard time getting excited about meeting strangers. It seemed so daunting.

"It's going to be your first date in, like, three years, so perk up."

"I'm perky. All perked. Can't wait."

"He knows what you do for a living because he asked me—well, you—after I asked him—well, you asked him—what he does."

"This is very confusing," I told her.

"I know. I've learned a lot, though. Like I learned that telling people I'm not really you right off the bat is not a good idea."

"Wait, what? What happened?" I asked, laughing.

"Well, with a few of the guys who seemed really awesome, I thought that being honest might be a good way to go, so I told them that I wasn't really you but that I was a good friend of yours and I was helping you find the right guy because you're too busy to do it yourself . . ."

"And that didn't go over so great?"

"No, not at all," she continued, laughing. "They got creeped out. One of them wrote back that he wasn't really into talking to someone's friend. Another one just never wrote back. And the other one asked me for a picture of myself . . . naked."

"Oh my God," I said, tearing up from laughing, "that's amazing."

"I know."

We got off the phone shortly after, but not before she reminded me that I had a date that week with a guy named Robert and that he'd be texting me later that day to set up the when and the where.

When I got the text, I responded, "Wednesday night would be great for me. Does that work for you?"

"That's perfect! Does eight o'clock work?"

*Yay! A normal first-date time.* "That works great."

"Awesome. Do you know El Carmen on Third Street? Great margaritas, good ambience," he responded.

*I love El Carmen! I love margaritas!* I thought. "I love El Carmen! I love margaritas," I wrote back.

"Ha, me too. Okay see you then."

"See you then!"

Okay, this was going a little better. He picked a great place to meet: El Carmen is a quiet, semidark little restaurant with a great bar—the perfect place to sit and talk while having a nice stiff drink to take the edge off the fact that you're meeting someone for the first time. Also, he didn't try to make me talk to him on the phone. He took care of business and then ended the texting, so we didn't have to continue on with some awkward "So what's up?" texts to each other.

Tilley was happy to hear that it sounded like her second attempt at sending me on a date was going a little more smoothly.

"Just don't have sex with him," she said very seriously.

"We're meeting at El Carmen for a margarita! How did you go to sex from that?"

"I've had their margaritas."

"Solid point. But he lives in Santa Monica and I live in Studio City. We're meeting in neutral territory, like twenty minutes from either of our houses. I wouldn't drive twenty minutes for sex with someone I just met."

Wednesday night came and I headed over to El Carmen to meet up with Robert. I wasn't dreading it as much as I thought I would. I'm even willing to admit that I was a little excited. Tilley had sent me the photos from his profile page, so I spotted him right away when I walked in. The real-life version of Robert resembled the profile pictures of Robert, except that he was much thinner and nerdier in person. He was cute; he just wasn't as ruggedly handsome as his profile photos suggested. I suspect those photos were taken a few years prior to that evening, but it didn't really bother me much. You sort of expect that from people now that Instagram filters give people digital tans and face-lifts.

"Robert?" I asked as I approached real-life Robert.

"Hey, Sarah," he said as he turned around to greet me. "Wow. You're even prettier in person."

"Oh, thank you," I said, blushing. Then I realized I didn't even know what pictures of me Tilley had posted on my profile page. She must have used one that was just okay, so that I wouldn't disappoint anyone in person; that seemed like the sort of crazy strategy The Advisor would come up with.

"Well, it's nice to meet you," Robert said as he offered the stool next to him.

I saw the bartender look up and blushed again. I instantly remembered how many times during my seventy-seven years of bartending I'd heard people meet for the first time in what was clearly an online date. I always made fun of them a little in my head. And now here I was, thirty-nine years old, having a bartender do the exact same thing to me. Oh, karma.

We both ordered margaritas and started the usual first-date banter. Talking about what we do for a living, where we're from, how long we've lived where we live now, blah blah blah. It was painless for the most part, once the initial awkwardness began to fade. The strong drink helped.

As we moved on to our second round of drinks, the conversation shifted to dating. Robert asked me how long I'd been on Match.com.

*So that's the website I'm on,* I thought. "Not long," I admitted. "This is actually the first date I've gone on from it."

"Oh, wow," he laughed.

"How long have you been on it?" I asked.

"Oh, years," he said nonchalantly.

*"Years?"* I repeated, not sure I'd heard him correctly.

"Yeah, years. Like five years or so? It really works."

I wasn't quite sure I was following his logic. If he had been on this dating website for five years and was still going on first dates, I don't think it "really works"—unless he just really loved going on first dates.

"What do you mean by that?" I asked, trying to figure out what his deal was without stating the obvious: that it wasn't really working for him.

"Well, I've been in three long-term relationships with people I've met on Match," he said proudly.

"Oh, that's . . . cool," I said, still not quite sure how he figured this was a success—unless he just really loves long-term relationships that eventually end.

"Yeah. I was with one girl for eight months, one girl for nine months, and my last girlfriend from Match and I moved in together after a couple of months and were together for ten."

"Well, hey, at least you added a month with each new relationship!" I said, laughing.

"Huh?" he asked blankly.

"Oh. Um, you said one was eight months, one nine, and the other ten . . . so I was just saying that each one gets a month longer."

"Huh, I'd never even thought of that," he said, very serious.

"Oh." *Well, I caught it right away.*

We continued on with the dating talk, him telling me why each of his "long-term" (is eight to ten months really that "long-term"?) relationships had ended. I won't bore you with the stories; for the most part it sounded like they just fizzled out.

"So how do you think this date is going?" he asked.

"What?"

"How's this going?"

"Oh, I—fine. Good. It's good."

"Sorry, was that a weird thing to ask?"

"Kind of," I admitted.

"Sorry. That's just kind of my thing. Like when a girl doesn't want to go on a second date with me, I always ask them why."

"That's weird. If someone doesn't want to go on a second date with me, I don't want to know why. I just assume it's their problem . . . it's more fun that way."

"Oh, not me. I really like feedback," he said enthusiastically.

Okay, so this guy definitely seemed a little strange, but it was kind of entertaining.

"All right, so what's some of the 'feedback' you've received?" I asked, really wanting to know.

"Well, one girl told me she didn't like that I'd been on Match for so long. One girl told me she thought I had a weird, creepy, low-talking voice, and another girl told me she just didn't really like my face," he said, smiling.

"Wow," I laughed, "that last girl sounds a little mean. But you seem to take it all very well."

"Yeah, I think it's really interesting."

Fuck. Now I was focused on his voice. *Why did he have to tell me that?*

"Well, you certainly don't have a creepy, low-talking voice," I said, lying.

"Well, that's good."

It *was* very low-talking and maybe a little creepy. I needed to end the date so that I didn't let it overwhelm me. We'd had some laughs and decent conversation; I didn't want to get too focused on one thing because it might make me not want to go on a second date with him and I was trying to be more open, per my friends' instructions.

"I should get going," I told him. "It's getting late." I wasn't lying. We had been there for three hours.

"You sure you don't want to have one more drink? We've only had two."

"No, I'm driving."

"Fair enough."

He walked me to my car and went in for a hug. "I'd like to do this again," he said after he pulled back.

"Me too. Mostly because I don't want you to ask me what's wrong with you," I teased.

He laughed and then went in for an awkward kiss. I didn't open my mouth so it was just a weird peck on the lips, like what you give your grandma or something.

When I got home, I texted Tilley to let her know that the date was okay, that he was a little weird, but that I would go out with him again.

"Well, that's better than nothing. I'm just relieved it wasn't a disaster," she responded.

"Not a disaster," I wrote back.

"Good. Thomas and I were worried if you had a terrible date you'd fire us."

"I can't believe you don't want to be fired."

"No way. It's so much fun."

"You two are insane. I'll talk to you tomorrow."

The next day I got a text from Robert, letting me know he had a good time and asking me how my day was.

"It's good, thanks. How's yours?"

"Great. So—about that second date. You around this week-end?"

"No, I have to go to Jacksonville for work," I told him.

"Oh, cool. You doing shows there?"

"Yeah, I've never performed in Jacksonville before. You ever been there?"

"No, but I've heard it's terrible."

"Great. I'm really looking forward to it now, thanks."

"Haha, sorry."

"I'm teasing," I responded. "I'll text you when I get back to see if we can meet up next week or something."

I went off to Jacksonville that weekend to perform. It definitely isn't the most exciting place in the world, but I had a good time. As much as I might complain about all the traveling I do for work, I actually love it. I always meet some fun people, whether they're from the audience or they work at the club. And there's never a lack of good old-fashioned people-watching.

I also always get out and wander the city a little. I'm very, very jealous of comedians who sleep in all day. I would love to do that. I'm just not a great sleeper. I work late and get up early. This is probably why I need a lot of under-eye concealer.

"How's Jacksonville?" a text from Robert inquired as I sat in my hotel room doing a crossword puzzle like an old lady.

"Amazing. Greatest city in the world," I replied.

"I knew it. How's the weather there?"

"It's rainy and cold."

"Ah, that sucks. It's like ninety and sunny here," he replied.

"That's why I love California," I replied. "How's your day?" I asked, moving us on from weather conversation.

"It's good. How's yours?"

"Good. I'm just getting some work done right now."

"Cool. So do you ever hook up with dudes when you're on the road?"

*Well, that escalated quickly,* I thought. Maybe I should have stuck with the weather conversation.

I looked at the phone for a minute, unsure how to respond. We barely knew each other. And despite my profession and the kind of my material I perform, I'm still a girl—and this felt like a weird area of questioning from someone I had been on one date with. So, I just responded with the truth (minus "Get that dick" guy).

"No. When I'm on the road I'm working. So I'm not really out meeting 'dudes,'" I wrote back.

"Oh, that's disappointing," he replied. "I was hoping for something a little more lurid than that."

Now I really had no idea how to respond. All I could think

about was his saying "lurid" in his creepy, low-talking voice. And I also decided that he was texting me pantsless, hoping to get some jerk-off material out of me.

So . . . I just didn't respond at all. Later that night, he texted me again and just said to let him know when I was back in town. I didn't respond to that either.

I know I promised to be more open, but his text totally turned me off. I ran it by Tilley, as I wanted her blessing to move on, which I received.

I never heard from Robert again. He obviously got the hint; he is a professional dater after all. But I've always been a little offended he never asked me what was wrong with him.

## New Year's . . . in Iowa

I don't really worry about New Year's Eve because I don't care much about celebrating it with anything more than a glass of champagne. It hasn't ever been a big deal to me, thankfully, because I know it can be a big bummer to a lot of single people. I prefer to get stressed out over more important things when single, like filling out the "emergency contact" part of the form at the doctor's office or worrying who is going to plan my funeral. But Christmas is the time of year that I can always take a real break without the worry of missing any work, because all of Hollywood shuts down until after the New Year, so during the upcoming 2013 holiday season, I was bound and determined to make sure I got my annual vacation in.

As I was Googling "safe places for a woman to vacation by herself without getting her head cut off," an e-mail came in from my agent with an offer to work on New Year's Eve.

*Oh, thank God,* I thought as I clicked to open the e-mail.

*I don't have to find anywhere to go, I'll turn wherever this offer is into my vacation!* I'd done stand-up on New Year's before and it's usually a lot of fun. It's a big night out for people and they're in a celebratory mood. Plus, clubs offer a lot of money for you to work because they know they're going to make it up in ticket and alcohol sales.

"Offer for NYE in Burlington, Iowa, at the PZAZZ! casino . . . " the e-mail read.

I frowned. *Where the fuck is Burlington, Iowa? Where the fuck is Iowa?*

I scanned down farther to see the money on the offer and decided that I'd probably be going to Burlington, Iowa, for New Year's Eve. Then I scanned even further down to see that the offer was to co-headline with Josh Wolf and decided that I'd definitely be going to Burlington, Iowa, for New Year's Eve.

Josh and I have been friends for about fifteen years. I didn't know anything about Burlington, Iowa, or a casino that didn't understand how to spell "Pizzazz," but I figured this could be an entertaining way to spend New Year's; the show was at eight o'clock and we only had to do one. We'd be free to hang out and wander around this weird casino afterward. *Plus*, I would be working, so I wouldn't have to explain to anyone that I really don't mind being alone on New Year's. Seriously, I don't. But other people look at you with such pity that they almost convince you there's something wrong with you just because you don't want to go out and deal with all the people who can't handle their alcohol.

It reminds me of the time I was on the phone with my mom and I told her I went to the movies alone. She was baffled, worried.

"Don't you have any friends out there?" she asked, her voice quivering.

"Yes, I have tons of friends out here, Mom. I just like going to the movies by myself sometimes. It's nice."

"Well. I don't understand that."

"Well, I could have gone with someone, and sometimes I do. But also sometimes I just like to go alone, okay?"

"Okay," she said, even though I could tell she definitely did not think it was okay.

If any of you haven't tried going to the movies alone, I suggest you do. It's not like I do it because I'm single; I've gone to the movies alone when I'm in a relationship, too. It's just a nice escape, time to zone out. Plus, nobody talks to you during the film, nobody puts their grubby hands in your popcorn, and nobody judges you for bringing in airplane bottles of vodka to spike your lemonade with.

Anyway, I texted Josh to confirm that he would be taking the New Year's Eve gig.

"Definitely. Beth is going to come, too."

A pang of disappointment hit me. Beth, Josh's wife, is awesome. I love her. I might even like her more than I like Josh (unless you're reading this, Josh, in which case I'm just saying that), but the second I realized he would be with his wife I felt very much like I was going to end up a third wheel.

"Okay, cool," I lied. "But I'm obviously not bringing any-one to Burlington. So you guys have to let me hang out with you after the show, up until the point where you want to go do it, in which case I don't expect to be invited."

"Of course you'll hang out with us, Beth already said for you not to worry about that . . ."

Ah, I love Beth. Even though she's married, she knows how to think like a single woman and she knew I'd be concerned.

"I mean, have you looked that place up? It's not like any of us are going anywhere else that night. It's in the middle of nowhere," he continued.

"I did look it up. And yes, we will be trapped there—probably under a few feet of snow."

We both agreed that regardless of location, it was worth the money and might make for a good story. So now I just had to figure out the rest of my trip. As I looked at a map of the United States, because I really did need to remind myself where Iowa was, I realized that if I went to Arkansas for Christmas, which I had to or my mom would faint from sadness, I pretty much had to stay there through my birthday in order to get to Burlington on December 30 (the casino requested that I get in the night before in case of bad weather or delays). The only thing between Arkansas and Iowa was Missouri, and I had no intention of spending my birthday there. The only other logi-cal thing I could see as an option for leaving Arkansas before my birthday was to get to the PZAZZ! casino even earlier and spend it there. But I would already have one night there alone

(Josh had somehow bullied them into letting him arrive the day of the show; apparently I need to be more aggressive), which I was kind of looking forward to after a week at my mom's house and all the constant talking that goes on there. But two nights alone in Burlington sounded like a suicide mission. So I slowly accepted that for the first time in about sixteen years, I was going to have to spend my birthday in Arkansas.

Around this same time, I also received an invitation to my friend Evan's wedding in Dallas, which would take place mid-January. Ugh, for someone who is okay with being single, my patience was really being tested. I definitely wanted to go to the wedding; I was never going to let the "I don't have a date" excuse keep me from anything important or fun. But, even though he and I are close, I was pretty sure I didn't know any of his friends. I imagined myself in Dallas, at the reception, at a table full of strangers, and I cringed. Could I do it? *Of course.* Did I want to? Not necessarily. I was invited with a "plus one," with Evan encouraging me to bring a friend if I wanted to. He was aware that I wouldn't know anyone at the reception, and we were both aware he probably wouldn't be able to hang out with me the entire time, since it was his wedding and all. But it felt weird to drag a girlfriend to Dallas for a wedding.

*I'm an adult,* I thought. *I can do this . . .*

Then I remembered that a girl I'd made friends with over the past couple of years, Lacy, lived in Dallas. And she actually knew Evan, too.

*. . . But I don't have to do this. I can bring Lacy!*

I quickly texted Lacy and she was very excited to respond that yes, she would love to be my platonic wedding date. She'd had a baby just a few months prior, so she was looking forward to having a night out.

*Problem solved.*

Shortly after I settled my wedding-date dilemma, Josh texted me to let me know that Beth would no longer be joining him in Burlington.

"Why not?" I asked, now kind of disappointed because the three of us would have had a ton of fun.

"Because it's Burlington. She loves me, but she's not an idiot."

"No, she's not," I wrote back, now excited again because I for sure wouldn't be a third wheel. I know a couple sentences ago I was disappointed, you guys. Being single around the holidays can be a real emotional roller coaster.

My trip home for Christmas is always something I look forward to, because I do get to see all of my family—Mom, Eric, sister, nephew, aunts, uncles, cousins. (Three out of four of them are married with kids, the fourth is engaged, and I used to babysit all of them. Luckily, they're smart enough not to ask me when I'm getting married.) I also always know that after about four days at my mom's house with dial-up Internet and never enough alcohol, I get a little (extremely) antsy (bitchy)—and this time I was going to be there for eight whole days . . . turning thirty-nine, single, in my parents' house.

The trip actually turned out to be really fun, as it usually does. I went to Christmas Eve service at my mom and Eric's church, which I've been doing for the past several years. When I was in my twenties, I'd be bratty and not attend. There wasn't a good reason for me to not want to go; I think I was just being defiant. *You can't make me do anything I don't want to do. I'm an adult!* Then one year I decided to go and I saw how much it meant to my mom that I did. On top of that, I really, really enjoyed going. It's the same church I went to when I was younger and it's beautiful. At the end of the service, the choir sings "Silent Night" while everyone in the church passes a lit candle to the person next to them to light theirs. By the end of the service, the entire church is glowing with candles and I always cry, even when I'm not on my period. So now it's something I look forward to. See? I have grown up a little.

After the service, we (my mom, stepdad, sister, and nephew) always watch a movie. I had brought some movie screeners that I'd gotten from the Writers Guild and Screen Actors Guild for "consideration" during award season. It always makes me feel super important to bring movies back home that aren't out on DVD yet. Since my nephew was there, I suggested we watch *Captain Phillips*. It was PG-13 and suitable for the whole family. Also, I had already seen it and loved it, and was pretty sure they all would, too.

Unfortunately, my stepdad doesn't have the best hearing, so he usually struggles a bit when we watch a movie at home. Closed-captioning is usually a lifesaver for him, but in the case of *Captain Phillips*, not so much. He spent a lot of the time trying to understand what the pirates were saying, my mom spent a lot of time trying to tell him, and my sister and I spent a lot of time laughing at the situation. That is, until the end of the movie, when my sister and I cried our eyes out because *oh my God Tom Hanks is so good*. Don't even get me started on my "I can't believe Tom Hanks wasn't nominated for an Oscar for *Captain Phillips*" rant right now because this book will take an ugly turn. Just know that I'm not fucking happy about his Oscar snub and if I knew who was responsible for it, that person and I would have a pretty serious conversation.

Anyway, as I looked around the living room that night, at my stepdad falling asleep in his recliner, my mom falling asleep in her spot on the couch with Elektra curled up in her lap, my nephew half watching the movie/half playing a game on his phone, and my sister curled up in a blanket crying, a big wave of happiness washed over me.

*I'm not turning thirty-nine alone,* I reminded myself. *I have them.*

The rest of the trip was nice and smooth. My sister and I realized that we never do anything with just the two of us, so we went on a "sister date" to *Anchorman 2*, followed by dinner at our mutually favorite local restaurant. I got to spend a lot of time with my nephew and the new golf clubs I surprised him with for Christmas. We all went to a basketball game. I hung out with my cousins and their babies. And, because of where my mom works, I attended a birthday party for one of her coworkers at the funeral home. Jealous?

The night of my birthday, the whole family went out to dinner. That used to be a pretty big number, but now that my cousins are married, it's even bigger, so when we go out to dinner there are like twenty of us. It sounds like a hassle in my head and then I go and realize how awesome it is that everyone still gets together to celebrate one another's birthdays. It's that grown-up thing again, I guess. After dinner, I met a few friends out for drinks. It was all very nice but low-key, and when I woke up the next day to leave for Iowa, I realized I had managed to seamlessly turn thirty-nine.

Once I settled into my room at the PZAZZ! hotel and casino, I decided I would wander out into the casino, have a drink, and maybe play some blackjack. I could do whatever I wanted to! I was on my own! Hooray!

This casino was a disaster. It definitely wasn't a Vegas casino—it was an Iowa casino. Although, I'm not sure one is better than the other. There was a permanent cloud of smoke hanging below the ceiling. The games all looked a little worn down, and so did the people. But I grew up in Arkansas. So this was my kind of place.

I had a fantasy of a steak dinner, so I wandered by the restaurant, only to find that it was a café and steak really was just a fantasy. So then I wandered up to the bar, ordered a drink, and sat down at a *Wheel of Fortune* machine. I was just about to put a twenty-dollar bill in and go off when a guy approached me and asked if I was Sarah from *Chelsea Lately*.

"I am." I smiled.

"What are you doing here?" he asked, looking confused.

"Oh, I'm performing here tomorrow night. You should come!"

"Oh, cool! Maybe I will!"

"Great! It'll be a good show. Josh Wolf is performing, too."

"Oh, awesome! Is he here?"

"No, he'll be here tomorrow," I said as I turned back to the *Wheel of Fortune* machine.

"Oh. So you're alone?" he whispered.

My back straightened. I paused, trying to figure out how to respond to this semi-creepy question.

"Nope, my friend is in the room right now," I lied.

"Oh," he sighed. I couldn't tell if he was disappointed because he wanted to hang out, have sex, or kill me.

"I better go check on him," I said as I jumped up and made a beeline for my room.

Look, I have no idea what this guy's motives were. It could have just been a simple, harmless observation on his part that I was alone. But I wasn't sticking around to find out.

So I spent the rest of my evening in the hotel room. Since the steak option wasn't one, I ordered a Reuben sandwich and a bottle of wine from room service, lay in bed, and watched bad TV all night. Honestly, it was wonderful.

Josh arrived late the next day. The casino manager, who looked exactly like Tom Arnold, took great care of us. He set up a whole spread in the green room—way more food than the two of us could ever get through, or so we thought. And the show went great. It was completely packed and the crowd was really fun. Afterward, while we were doing the usual meet-and-greet with the audience, Josh asked me if I wanted some edible pot. Now, to be clear, I'm not very good high, so I don't get high very often at all. It makes me unable to hold a conversation and I just end up staring at people and giggling to myself. When my best friend got married years ago, someone gave me a medical marijuana pill that I think was meant for a horse. I was so stoned that all I did was sit in a corner and make a sound that I can only compare to what it sounds like when you try to stifle a sneeze. And the last time I'd gotten high prior to Josh's offer was probably about a year earlier. I was at a party at a friend's house and there was a guy there whom I had a pretty big crush on. Everyone else was high so I decided, *Why not?* Cut to me talking to the guy I had a crush on for a good half hour, then getting really quiet for about five straight minutes, then breaking the silence by asking him, "So what are you doing this summer?" This took place in January.

"Why not?" I responded to Josh, totally ignoring the part of my brain that knew better.

As the edible chocolate concoction set in, Josh and I headed out to roam the casino.

"I think I'm really high," I said to Josh as we rounded a corner to scope out the gambling situation.

"All right, then you probably don't need the other half of that chocolate," he told me.

"Wait . . . other half?"

"You mean you ate the whole thing?"

"Was I not supposed to?"

"Too late now," Josh laughed. "This is going to be hilarious."

A couple of girls who had been at the show spotted us and started walking our way.

"Oh, no," I said, panicked.

"What?" Josh asked.

"People."

As the two girls got closer, I looked around for a place to escape, but there was nowhere to go.

"Hey, guys! We loved the show!" one of the girls said excitedly.

"Thank you!" Josh replied.

I just stared at them.

"So what are you guys doing now? Can we buy you shots?"

Josh looked at me, then back at the girls. "No, thank you. We both have early flights tomorrow."

"Oh, come on! It's New Year's Eve!" the other girl said encouragingly.

"Eeeeeve," I giggled.

"What?" the girls asked in unison.

"Candy," I replied.

Both girls looked completely confused and I thought that was hysterical. Josh thanked them again for coming to the show, then grabbed my elbow and led me away before I could make a complete asshole out of myself.

I was still laughing about the word "Eve" when I looked up and saw a sign that said CANDY ALLEY. For a second I thought I was hallucinating, but when I pointed to the sign, Josh got really excited, so I knew that the sign was there and that it really was pointing us to a place called Candy Alley.

That night, Candy Alley was the best place I'd ever set foot in. It had every kind of candy imaginable. There was a girl behind the counter and you just told her what you wanted and she scooped it into a bag. I did a lot of pointing and she did a lot of scooping, but she remained very pleasant—she probably thought it was nice that the dark-haired gentleman I was with took his mentally challenged sister out for some candy on New Year's.

Once Josh and I were both armed with giant bags of candy, we headed back to my room and turned on the television. We laughed about the girls and what an idiot they must have thought I was. Stuffing my face with candy and laughing with my good friend turned out to be the perfect way to spend New Year's. We didn't even make it until midnight together, though, both of us wanting to lie in bed and watch TV alone for the remainder of the evening. So around eleven o'clock, Josh went back to his room. I immediately crawled into bed, ready to flip back and forth between New Year's countdown shows and re-runs of *Bar Rescue*. But something was missing. So I got up and slowly cracked open my door, looked both ways to make sure I wouldn't have to encounter another person (including Josh), then ran to the green room to see if any of that food the manager had ordered for us was still there. Unfortunately, it was. So I grabbed a plate and piled on enough cheese to kill someone, then darted back to my room. When I got in my room, I realized I was not wearing pants, so it really was a good thing I hadn't run into anyone else.

The next morning, I checked out of the hotel feeling pretty good, because I was no longer high *and* I was wearing pants. The nice lady at the front desk told me that the car service would pick me up at nine o'clock. I looked around and didn't see a town car outside, so I asked the lady at the front desk if she knew where the ride for Sarah Colonna was.

"Right here!" I heard a voice call out from behind me.

I turned to see an elderly couple standing by the entrance to the hotel.

"You ready to go?" the man asked.

"Um, okay," I said, totally confused as he pointed to his Toyota Corolla, which was just on the other side of the glass doors.

Look, I'm not a diva or anything, so don't judge me—but what the fuck? Even most comedy clubs send a town car for you to and from the airport, and every casino I've ever performed in definitely has. This just seemed like I was getting a ride to the airport from someone's grandparents.

*What kind of operation are they running here?* I wondered as I lifted my own bags into the trunk because I was worried that my giant suitcase might be too much for the eighty-year old man who was about to drive me to the airport.

I noticed that the man was very tall, so I started to get in the backseat behind his wife.

"Oh, no, sorry—there's a car seat there. My grandson's." She smiled.

"Oh, okay. I'll get in on the other side."

The old man was taller than I thought; his seat was so far back that my knees were basically resting on my boobs. Luckily, the airport was only an hour and a half away. FML.

It was snowing and the woman kept telling her husband to keep his eyes on the road. It seemed like he was looking straight ahead, so unless his eyes were closed, he seemed to have them on the road. But this felt as if it was their usual banter so I just tried to tune it out.

"So you're a magician?" the old man asked me.

"Huh?"

"We heard you're a magician. You put on a magic show last night, right?" he asked.

"Um, no. I'm not a ma— Yeah, I'm a magician," I said, surrendering. The last thing I wanted to hear right then was, "A comedian?! Well, then tell us something funny!"

"Oh, can you show us a magic trick?" the wife asked.

*Crap, I didn't think of that.*

"Um, I can't do magic tricks in a car," I told them in a very serious tone.

"Oh. Well, can you do a small trick?" she asked.

I looked at her and really wished I knew at least one small magic trick—to make her happy and to get her off my ass—but I don't know any magic tricks. Nothing.

"My powers don't work in moving vehicles," I explained.

"Oh, I guess that makes sense," the man said.

*It does?*

"Well, did you have a nice evening last night? After your magic show?" the woman asked me, still trying to make small talk.

"It was nice," I said, opting not to tell them that I ended my night eating cheese pantsless in bed. The memory of the cheese made my stomach hurt and I winced.

"You feel okay?" she asked, noticing my grimace.

"Oh, Martha, she probably had a couple of daiquiris last night, it was New Year's Eve. Let her be."

"Yeah, I had one too many daiquiris," I agreed, wondering if people still drank daiquiris anywhere except at TGI Fridays.

Everyone got quiet and I pretended to fall asleep to avoid any more questions. While I "slept," they had a ninety-minute conversation about Steak 'n Shake.

When I got to the airport, I texted Josh to let him know that he would not be getting picked up by a car service but instead by two people who reminded me of the old couple from *Mulholland Drive.*

"Good luck with that," I wrote.

"Oh, Jesus," he responded. "Did you go back out to the casino after I left your room? I could have sworn I heard your door open and shut."

"Nope, must've been the person on the other side of you," I told him. He didn't need to know about the cheese incident. I wanted to try to leave Iowa with a little bit of dignity.

A few plane-deicing (is that really safe?) delays later, I was alone, back in the comfort of my home in Los Angeles. It was the first day of the New Year and so far nothing had changed, but I was determined that it was going to.

## Table for Dos

Although I was disappointed and/or creeped out by the first couple of men I encountered via Tilley Dating Services, I remained open and optimistic. I figured I didn't have much to lose, especially since Tilley was doing all of the legwork.

Meanwhile, I was off to Evan's wedding in Dallas. I decided not to drag my wedding date, Lacy, to the rehearsal dinner. I felt like taking her to both things would definitely secure my lesbian status among the rest of the wedding guests and I didn't want to kill all possibility of having a weekend wedding fling. I wasn't *planning* on having a weekend wedding fling, but I wasn't *not* planning on it either. I wanted to keep my options open.

The rehearsal dinner was held at a trendy Dallas restaurant that Evan had rented out for the evening. On the taxi ride over, I pictured my entrance: me walking in alone, into a crowd of family and friends, all of whom knew each other, laughing and carrying on, catching up. Married couples sharing stories with the bride and groom, telling them what to expect in the months to come. Unmarried couples basking in the glow of the soon-to-be-wed couple, soaking up the romantic tale of how they came to be engaged, with excitement and nervousness, wondering if they are next. Then me, alone and out of my element, carrying an extra five pounds in water weight because God decided to give me my period for the wedding in hopes to deter me from having sexual activity with a stranger, elbowing my way to the bar.

A man in a suit stopped me at the entrance.

*Oh, here we go,* I thought as I pulled my pashmina off just enough to give the nice man a glimpse of my cleavage.

*I guess even with five extra pounds I look pretty good in this dress.*

"Sorry, ma'am, the restaurant is closed for a private event," he said, stepping in front of the door as if I was a terrorist.

"Yeah, for a rehearsal dinner, right? I'm here for that," I explained as I pulled my pashmina back over my breasts.

"Oh, sorry. Is it just you or are you waiting for someone to park the car?"

"Just me," I replied as I pulled the pashmina tighter.

"Just you?"

"Just me," I repeated as I blew past him and into the restaurant, "table for *uno.*"

Much to my relief, Evan and Gina were standing right by the entrance. So, I chatted with them for a couple of minutes, then went off to the bar to order some sort of concoction that Evan insisted was a house specialty. I don't know what was in it, but it looked and tasted like a piña colada, which seemed like an odd "specialty" for a trendy Dallas restaurant, but it had alcohol in it so I didn't really give a shit. A few minutes later, we were told to take our seats so that the first course could be served. Having already sucked down a couple of specialty drinks, I ordered myself a vodka martini and then looked around, unsure where to sit.

"You're at our table," Evan whispered to me as he motioned for me to follow him.

There were five seats at the table, for the bride-and-groom-to-be, another couple, and me. The couple immediately asked me where I was from and what I did for a living, and when I told them, they seemed very interested. They were armed with many questions about my career, about what it's like to do stand-up, and about what made me decide I wanted to be a comedian. Sometimes, that gets on my nerves. Maybe I don't like to talk about myself or maybe I just don't find it as interesting to talk about because to me, it's just my job—or maybe I'm just an asshole, I'm not sure. But that night, I was extremely happy to answer any and all questions they had about my job. I braced myself for questions about my personal life to follow, but they never came. They were either smart enough to know not to ask a woman alone at a rehearsal dinner such a thing, or they didn't give a shit. Either way, I was grateful to talk to people who didn't see me as a single woman in town alone for

242 --- *Sarah Colonna*

a wedding—they saw me as a woman with a career sitting next to them at a table. If I could have kissed them both on the lips without making everyone feel awkward, I would have.

The wedding itself was beautiful. I cried a little, just like I always do at weddings. There isn't one wedding that I've been to that I didn't cry during. After Sarah Tilley got married, she sent me a photo that was taken of me blubbering during the ceremony.

"You're such a softie," she said when she texted the picture to me.

"I always cry at weddings!" I said defensively. "But in this case I think I was just crying because I was so hungover." (This was a lie; I don't really get hangovers.)

Evan and Gina's reception was a blast, too, and Lacy was the perfect date. We sat at a table full of fun people and we always needed our drinks refilled at the same time. And the best part of all: nobody tried to make me go catch the fucking bouquet. All in all, for something I was slightly dreading, it turned out to be a solid weekend. On the flight home, I breathed a sigh of relief as I realized that I was still okay on my own. What had I gotten myself so worked up about in the first place?

A couple days after I got back to L.A., I noticed a tweet someone sent to me. It stood out as the sender said that he had met a friend/coworker of mine, Ross Mathews, at "the game on Sunday" and hoped Ross put in a good word for him with me. I clicked on the profile to see that it was a guy named Jon who plays for the Seattle Seahawks. Ross is a huge fan of the Seahawks, so his being at the game made sense to me. Although I am a fan of sports, football is the sport I follow the least, as it generally confuses the shit out of me. I did know the Seahawks were on their way to the Super Bowl, but that was about it. However, I was curious about this guy who wanted to meet me, so I Googled him.

*Oh, wow. He's so cute,* I thought as I navigated to his Wikipedia page. *And he's not married.*

*Oh, wow. He's really good at his job,* I thought as I scanned the page about his career. I didn't know what all of it meant, but I did know that it was impressive.

*Oh, wow. He's only thirty-two*, I thought as I read that he was born in 1981. *I wonder if he knows how old I am?* Surely he knew how old I was. Guys Google, too, right? *Right?* It's not as if it was a huge age difference, but I'm used to dating guys my age or older.

*But I've dated some pretty immature forty-year-olds,* I reminded myself. Let's not forget good ol' "Who Farted?"

I texted Ross and asked him what the deal was with this guy.

"I was at the game and he came up to me and said to put in a good word with you! So I told him to tweet to us. He's so cute!" Ross wrote back.

"Okay, so should I tweet him back?"

"YES! Season seats forever!"

Now, I'm sure you guys are all thinking, *Really? Another fucking guy on Twitter?* But at this point I don't see how it's different from Match.com or any other website. And since the last guy Tilley set me up with turned out to be some kind of weird voyeur, I figured what the hell. Plus, I knew Ross wouldn't steer me wrong, even for season tickets to the Seahawks. But just to be sure, I texted Tara and Stephanie, who I knew would (a) give me good advice, and (b) be super excited a football player tweeted me. They are both *huge* football fans—I mean, they're still baseball fans, too, just not quite as much since the whole chain-to-the-chin incident had occurred.

"I know who he is! He used to play for the Packers!" Steph wrote back, delirious with excitement that a guy who played for her favorite team of all time was flirting with me. "They cut him and all the fans were upset because he's one of the best punters in the league. I don't know why they cut him but it would be great if you could find out."

"What's a punter do?" I wrote back.

"He punts, dumbass," she replied. Then she went on to explain when a punter punts, why he punts, etc. I didn't understand a word of it.

"This is amazing," Tara chimed in (yes, we also three-way text—don't judge). "I just went to his Twitter page. Go to it and scroll down to a tweet that's dated November twenty-third of last year."

"When did you learn to use Twitter?" Steph replied.

"Just go look, assholes."

I followed instructions and went through Jon's timeline, which thankfully didn't take too long because he's not an over-active Twitter user.

"So bummed I missed @sarahcolonna in Seattle tonight, but she's an Angels fan, so hopefully I'll catch her in Tempe for Spring Training?"

I had performed just outside of Seattle the very night that he sent this tweet—in November. So here we were in January . . .

"He's obviously been trying to get your attention for a while!" Tara wrote back.

"*And he played for the Packers*," Steph reminded us.

"Okay, girls. I'm going to write him back. I'll keep you posted."

"I'm listening," I tweeted to Jon, trying to reply in a flirty manner about a "good word" being put in.

That tweet led to a few flirty tweets involving Ross officiating our wedding in a leotard while a Beyoncé song played (I pray that really happens one day). It was entertaining, but obviously silly, so after a couple of days of those exchanges, I wrote it off as a quick fun flirt.

But then a direct message from him popped up. "Here's my number so we can plan our wedding," he wrote. Which, again, was cute, but thus far there wasn't anything but flirty jokes. I couldn't tell if he was seriously interested in me.

"And yes, this is my super-awkward attempt at picking you up on Twitter. I didn't know how else to get in touch with you," said another message that followed.

Okay, that seemed like a real flirt—like he was actually interested and acknowledging the awkwardness of the situation. I alerted Steph and Tara of the progress and asked them how I should respond.

"Okay, so far it's all been jokes about your wedding and whatnot. So, I think in order for this to move forward, he needs to know you aren't just joking. So when you respond, don't mention anything about the wedding," Steph ordered.

"I agree," Tara chimed in. "Just say that his flirting worked. That way he has your number and if he's serious about wanting to meet you, he'll take it from there."

So later that night, I texted the number he had given me.

"Your attempt worked," I wrote, following orders from team Steph and Tara. "So now you have my number, too."

I didn't hear back from him that night, but the next morning I did.

"I'm really glad that worked. Sorry I didn't write you back last night, I'm in New York so I was in bed when you wrote me."

*Oh my God, that's right!* I remembered. He was in New York for the Super Bowl. I assumed that was a pretty big deal to him, and I thought it was kind of great that he was still thinking about me.

Our texts continued throughout that week. We were just kind of talking. It was weird, because we didn't know each other at all, but the texts flowed easily, as if we had been friends for years. At one point, he acknowledged that we hadn't spoken on the phone.

"Should I call you?" he asked. "I don't want to be rude, if I should call you I can . . ."

"I sort of hate talking on the phone," I replied. "Is that weird?"

"Oh thank God. I hate talking on the phone, too. I wish everything could be done via text."

"Me too!"

Okay, so we'd established that even though we had never met, we were both perfectly comfortable with communicating via text for now. I thought about the guy from Match.com whom I had that long, painful, nowhere conversation with and breathed a sigh of relief that I wasn't going to have one of those with Jon. If he was that boring or hard to talk to, I didn't want to know yet. I was having too much fun with what we had going on and I wasn't in the mood for it to be ruined already.

"So I know we've just been texting, but I really would like to take you on an actual date," he wrote to me one day.

"I'd love that," I replied.

"Well, I'm a little tied up until Sunday, but after that I'm wide open."

"Are you nervous?" I asked him. I couldn't imagine what it must be like to be preparing all week for what I assume is the biggest game of a football player's life.

"Yeah, a little. But I'm also just really excited. Are you going to watch the game?"

"Well, I'm going to a Super Bowl party at my friend Tara's house. I usually don't pay attention to the game much, but I have a feeling this time I will," I replied, followed by a "wink face" emoticon. I needed to get the emoticon usage out there. I can't control my love for them.

He replied with the "happy face blushing" emoticon.

"Sorry if I made you use an emoticon," I wrote back. "I'm sort of obsessed with them. I think they're hilarious."

"I'm glad you did. I love using them, but I usually hold off until the other person uses them first because I'm a grown man and all."

*He just keeps getting better,* I thought.

"I live in Phoenix in the off-season, but I am coming to California in a couple of weeks. I'm taking my nieces and nephews to Disneyland. Maybe I can take you out then? I'll be there for a few days."

"Ouch. Disneyland. That sounds awful," I replied. "But I'd love for you to take me out."

"I know! I have so many nieces and nephews. They all live in Canada and they are dying to go to Disneyland. It sounds like a nightmare but they'll be happy. I'm just grateful my brother and sisters had so many kids because that keeps my mom from bugging me about having them."

"You don't want kids?" I asked.

"No, I just never have. I like them and all, but I don't want any of my own."

*Was this guy created in a lab for me?*

The day of the Super Bowl, I went to the party Tara was having at her house. I arrived straight from the airport after doing shows in Philadelphia, so I was exhausted but very excited to watch the game. I'd never been excited to watch the game at a Super Bowl party before—usually I just show up for the cheese dip.

Right when I arrived, Steph and Tara took me aside to get the latest news on my text relationship with Jon.

"Well, this morning we were texting and basically I just told him good luck. He said thanks and then he said he was heading over to the field."

"He texted you today? The day of the Super Bowl?" Steph exclaimed.

"He loves you," Tara said.

"I think he was just being nice because I had said—"

"Football players aren't ever just being nice," Steph explained. "I agree with Tara, he loves you."

"Okay, well we haven't even met yet so let's all calm down. We've been hurt by this kind of situation before."

"When are you meeting?" Tara asked, interrogating me.

"He's taking his nieces and nephews to Disneyland in a couple of weeks, so I think he's going to come up to L.A. and take me out."

"That's so cute that he's taking his family to Disneyland! Plus, that's what you're supposed to do after the Super Bowl, so that means he knows they're going to win!" Steph exclaimed.

"Huh? Who goes to Disneyland after they win the Super Bowl?" I asked, clueless.

"Hello? You've never seen the commercials?" Tara asked.

"What commercials?"

"The 'I'm going to Disneyland' commercials. What, do you live under a rock?" Steph asked.

"Oh, I've totally seen those," I lied.

"Wait, so does he want kids?" Tara asked.

"No, he told me he doesn't."

"Oh thank God," she said, looking at Steph with a relieved glance.

"What was that glance about?"

"Tara was worried that since he's thirty-two he might want kids and since you don't, it might end up being a deal-breaker for you guys."

"You two talked about whether or not he wants to have kids? We haven't even met yet. I think you guys need to take it down a notch. You're getting too invested in this; I don't want you two to end up heartbroken."

"We just have a good feeling about it," Tara explained.

*"Plus, he used to play for the Packers!"* Steph yelled.

That day, I watched more of a football game than I ever had in my life.

When it was time for Jon to finally punt, the girls told me to get ready to watch.

"Great, I'll go make us fresh drinks so we can toast after he punts!" I said excitedly as I headed to the kitchen to get some ice.

"Stop, dumbass. This isn't baseball, he's up right now," Steph told me as she pointed toward the screen.

"Oh," I said as I focused my attention back toward the television.

He only punted once, but when he did apparently it was very, very good. (I had to ask because just watching it told me nothing.)

"Why isn't he playing more?" I asked after his one and only punt. "Does the team not like him or something?"

"What? It's because it's a blowout. They don't need him to," Steph explained.

"I don't understand this game," I sighed.

"Well, you better start understanding. You can't be an NFL wife and not know what the fuck is going on," she said, scolding me.

"So now I'm marrying him? We haven't even met."

"Don't ruin my day," she said as she handed me a Jell-O shot that I awkwardly tried to get in my mouth. It's not easy.

An hour or so after the game, I received a text from Jon, shirtless, in the locker room, holding the team's trophy in his hand. "Champions!" it said.

"Oh my God! Look!" I yelled as I motioned for Steph and Tara to come over.

"Oh my God!" Steph repeated. "He texted you right after he won the Super Bowl!"

"He loves you," Tara said insistently.

I was actually just thinking about how good he looked shirtless. But then I realized they had a point. I received several random texts from Jon throughout the night, updating me on what sort of shenanigans ensued post–Super Bowl win. I have to admit, I was really taken by surprise that he thought to text me. I mean, I had realized over the past couple of weeks that he seemed genuinely interested, but I assumed after winning a championship like that, single (and unfortunately, probably also married) guys walked around the city with their dicks out.

Over the next couple of weeks, Jon and I continued our constant texting. We would text about our day, our night, whatever. We would text that we missed each other, acknowledging that it was odd since we hadn't even met. It felt very normal—like we had known each other forever and texting every day was a part of our usual activity.

Finally, the week of Jon's trip to Disneyland arrived. We'd decided that he'd come up to L.A. and take me out to dinner on Monday night. He told me he wanted to plan the date, but that he might need a little help, as he wasn't very familiar with the area. I loved that he wanted to plan it but also knew I better throw out a few restaurant suggestions because I certainly didn't want our first date to be at a shitty restaurant in the Valley.

"Do you have a favorite Italian restaurant?" he texted one night.

"I do! Italian is my favorite!"

"I figured it must be, with your last name and all . . ."

I suggested a couple of places and let him pick one.

"Okay, I made a reservation for eight o'clock at Ago," he informed me.

*I was really hoping he'd pick Ago,* I thought, smiling.

He had driven his family up from Phoenix in a large rented Escalade.

"I can't pick you up in this car, it's huge. It's too embarrassing," he wrote me the morning of our date.

"Oh, I don't care about that," I assured him.

"No, really. It's ridiculous. I can't pick you up in this."

"Well, I guess you could take an Uber up here? I don't know what it would cost . . ."

"Oh, I'm definitely doing that. If you don't mind?"

"Of course I don't mind, silly. Plus that way you can have a couple of drinks without worrying about driving," I wrote.

"I like the way you think."

I don't think it's ever taken me as long to get ready for a date as it did that night. I mean, I'm no makeup wizard and my hair basically does itself, so I didn't really spend any extra time on *that*—I put on the same two coats of eye shadow I've been putting on for twenty years, still consulting the back of the makeup case to figure out exactly how to apply to my eyelid "crease." But it took me a *really* long time to get dressed.

I decided to text Sarah Tilley, who technically was still in charge of my love life, to ask her what I should wear. She wasn't thrilled about the fact that I had met someone on my own and she was really not thrilled about the fact that it was a guy with a six-pack. So I wanted to give her *something*.

"Cute top, good butt-jeans, heels," she responded immediately. "And underwear, please wear underwear."

"I always wear underwear."

"Oh, that's right, that was me that used to not wear under-wear. But I do now."

"Well, that's great news," I responded.

"Are you going to have sex with him?" she asked.

"What? No! I mean . . . am I allowed to?"

"You can do whatever you want. If it's the right guy, having sex on the first date doesn't matter either way."

"I agree! But I think I'm going to not have sex with him. Mostly because I know he has to go back to Anaheim and I'd rather have sex when he can sleep over. It feels dirty when they leave after."

"True," she agreed.

"But if *I* leave after it's okay because that means I don't like the guy that much."

"Also true."

"I'm glad we agree."

"Have fun, whore," she said, signing off with her usual charm.

"Thanks. And, Tilley? I'm really sorry he has a six-pack."

"No you're not."

"You're right, I'm not."

I took Tilley's advice and put on a cute top, my best ass-jeans, and a pair of wedge heels—they're easier to walk in than regular heels, especially after a couple of drinks, and I certainly didn't want to take any humiliating tumbles on our first date. If we dated for long, he'd get to witness plenty of those, as bal-ance in general is not my strong suit. I changed my top about sixteen times, finally settling on a black top that showed a *little* cleavage but not *too* much cleavage. Having my tits totally out for a professional athlete seemed a little too typical. I really thought this shit through, you guys.

When he knocked on my door, my heart started pounding and I immediately began to sweat.

*Fuck. Why do I always sweat when I'm nervous?* I thought as I grabbed a towel and dabbed my face and armpits (I know, *classy*).

"Coming!" I yelled as I opened the door.

*Why did I just yell "coming" when I'm clearly already here?*

My heart skipped a beat. He was even more handsome in person than all of the images I had Googled—and I had Googled a lot of images of him.

"Hi." He smiled.

"Hi." I smiled back.

We stood there for a few seconds, or maybe it was ten minutes. Then he moved closer and kissed me. We kissed for a few seconds, or maybe it was ten minutes.

"I can't believe you're here," I said as we pulled apart.

"I can't either." He grinned.

"Oh my God, I'm so sorry, come in," I said as I moved out of the doorway. "Or do you just want to go? I can grab my purse."

"Well, I told the Uber driver we would be a few minutes because I brought you something," he said as he acknowledged a rather large bag in his hand.

We walked upstairs to my living room and I opened the gift he brought me, starting with the card.

"I feel like we know each other so well already but I just wanted to give you a few little things so you can get to know me a bit better . . . ," the card read.

As I opened the bag, I found several items inside.

"What's all this?" I asked as I pulled out DVDs, CDs, and candy.

"They're my favorite things." Jon smiled. "I'm excited to find out what your favorite things are, too."

*Oh my God, he's gay,* sarcastic Sarah crept into my mind to utter.

*Fuck off, he's just incredibly thoughtful and you're not used to that,* rational Sarah said insistently.

"This is amazing," I said as I took in each item. One of his favorite movies was *Bull Durham. Points.*

His favorite candy was Twizzlers. *I prefer Red Vines,* I thought. *This may never work.*

Then I pulled out a bottle of champagne—his favorite—Veuve Clicquot. *Okay, this is good; I can deal with the Twizzlers thing.*

"I love this champagne, too!" I smiled.

"Do you have any plastic cups? Let's pour a glass for the ride to the restaurant," he suggested.

If he proposed right then I would have probably said yes.

At the restaurant, it was very obvious we were smitten. At one point I asked him if it seemed like the table was wider than tables at other restaurants.

"I'm so glad you said that, I feel so far away from you and I hate it," he said as he held my hand from across the ocean-sized table between us.

I wanted to just go sit right next to him, but I had mocked too many "same sider" couples in my waitressing days to do so with a clear conscience. So instead, we sat suffering.

Jon ordered a bottle of Veuve, which I thought was something he was doing because it was a special occasion, but I would later find out that that's just what he likes to drink, regardless of the meal. What? Don't all six-foot-tall, buff NFL players order a glass of champagne with their lunch? If not, they should.

I think dinner was good, but neither of us was really paying attention to the food. We were lost in conversation, which thankfully came very easily for us. There's nothing worse than the silent first-date dinner. We polished off our champagne as the waiter approached.

"Any dessert for the lovebirds?" He smiled.

*Oh my God, we must look like such assholes,* I thought.

"Is it that obvious?" Jon laughed.

"You remind me of this older African-American couple that was in here before. They were so in love," the waiter replied.

As we waited outside for the Uber driver after dinner, I looked up at Jon.

"Did our waiter compare us to an elderly black couple?" I asked him.

"Oh, good, you caught that, too."

Later, when we got back to my place, my plan to maybe not have sex with him fell through. No, that's not the first time that's happened to me. But this time, it felt like waiting any longer would be complete torture—plus, we didn't even know when we would see each other again.

He had to leave around five o'clock in the morning in order to take his family to Disneyland. I heard from him on his way to Anaheim, when he got to Anaheim, and all throughout the day.

"I wish I could see you again before I leave," he wrote at one point, his thoughts mirroring mine.

I knew he wouldn't have time to make the hour-or-so trek back up to Los Angeles, so I offered to come down to meet him for a quick drink that night, before he had to head back to Phoenix.

We were probably just as disgusting to watch that night while we sat at a quiet dive bar just around the corner from his hotel. I'm sure I owe an apology to the many deliriously happy-looking couples I've rolled my eyes at over the years. Later that night, I dropped him off back at his hotel, having to make do with kissing good-bye because his room was connected to his family's room and any other sort of shenanigans on our part would have been a little bit rude.

"That's my move," I told him before he got out of the car, "I give it up on the first date, then hold out on the second."

He made a comment about how horrible it was that he couldn't take me upstairs and kissed me good night. I grinned like an asshole the whole drive home.

The next day, two dozen roses were delivered to my door. "I had the best time with you, I can't wait to see you again," the card read.

I immediately wrote him and thanked him, then took a picture of the roses and texted it to all of my girlfriends.

"Oh, he's good," every single one of them responded.

A couple weeks later, I had an annual girls' trip with Tara and Steph to Angels Spring Training, which just so happens to take place in Tempe, Arizona, which just so happens to be smack next to Phoenix. This was planned before I ever even spoke to Jon, and damn it, I have the reservation confirmation from the hotel to prove it. I knew that Jon was also a huge baseball fan and a fan of attending Spring Training games. I had mentioned my upcoming trip to him, but we both agreed I shouldn't be the girl who tries to bring a guy into the girls' trip. And he really didn't want to be the guy who crashed the girls' trip.

"Are you insane?" Tara asked as I quietly mentioned that he lived there and that maybe he could meet us out for a drink one night. "He should meet us every night. We are dying to meet him!"

"I concur!" Steph said excitedly. "Is he going to be okay with me asking him a couple of questions about when he played for Green Bay?"

"He's prepared for that," I laughed. Knowing how big a fan of Green Bay Steph is, I had already warned Jon that subject might come up if he met her.

Our conversation went from me explaining that I would not spend the night with him either night because it was a girls' trip and we needed to sing karaoke in our underwear with no boys around, to them bargaining with me to spend one night with him as long as I didn't leave out any details the next day.

Steph decided since this was a "new relationship" (her words, not mine—I was not yet calling it a relationship since so far we had only been on two dates), I was going to need to go see him right away when we got to Phoenix. She figured out that if I went to his place, she and Tara could find somewhere to have happy hour and he and I could meet up with them after we got some afternoon sex out of our systems.

"Really? I feel bad just going to see him right when I get there; this is our trip," I told them as we sucked down Bloody Marys at the airport.

"Don't be ridiculous, this is a new relationship, you need to have sex. You guys are all pent up," Tara chimed in.

"I know, but I'm going to see him next weekend all by myself," I explained as I drained my drink.

"What? You are? Oh my God, you guys are in love," Steph said.

"I didn't tell you? Yes. We decided since I have next weekend off, I should come back to Phoenix. I have to perform like every weekend after that for a while so it seemed like a good time to hang out."

"That's so awesome. But yes, you still need to see him when we get in," they said insistently.

Obviously, I wasn't going to argue with them about this. The truth was, I *didn't* want to be "that girl" who brought a guy into the trip, but I also really, really liked this guy. And I hadn't really liked someone—someone who was available and real and wasn't afraid to show me how much he liked me, too—in so long that I had almost forgotten how exciting it can be. I think that excitement bleeds onto the people who care about you and suddenly they're almost as caught up in it as you are.

The minute I walked into Jon's condo in Phoenix, we attacked each other like he had been off fighting a war for seven years. When we finally pulled it together, we left to go meet Steph and Tara at a bar down the street. We walked in to see they had ordered a bottle of Veuve for him, which Jon thought was both hilarious and sweet.

"Your hair looks insane," Steph laughed as we sat down.

"You look like you just took a quaalude," Tara said.

Jon and I both blushed.

"It's called an orgasm," Steph laughed.

And just like that Jon was thrown right into the fire with two of my closest friends.

"Well, then how does my hair look?" Jon asked.

We all laughed and the awkward "we just had sex and every-one at the table knows it" moment was put to rest (until he got up to go to the bathroom and they grilled me).

Tara and Steph loved Jon, as I knew/hoped they would, and vice versa. So, despite my attempts to play it cool, he ended up going to a game with us and joining us for dinner one night, and I ended up spending both nights at his place. We had all decided I'd only spend one night with him, but that changed on the second night after Steph had gone back to the hotel early because she wasn't feeling well and Tara drunkenly insisted that I stay with Jon because she was going to pass out, anyway—no girls'-night karaoke meant I might as well get some sex. The next morning, at eight o'clock, Jon shook me awake.

"Babe, babe, you have to get up!"

"What? Why? Wait—did you just call me 'babe'?"

"I did. Do you not like it?"

"No, I love it." I smiled. And I really did. I couldn't remember if anyone else had called me that before. I knew that Tori Spelling and Dean what's-his-face called each other "babe," so I never thought I'd want anyone to call me that. But suddenly I understood them.

"Okay, good. But we have to go. I can't be the guy who brings you back late. I promised them I'd have you back in time for you guys to have breakfast together!"

I grinned at how cute it was that he was so worried about my friends and what they thought. He was out to make a good impression and he wasn't going to let me ruin it, even though I tried to because I really just wanted to do it again, especially after the whole "babe" thing left me oddly aroused.

I made it back for breakfast as promised, then the girls and I went to another baseball game, and that night we headed home.

Thankfully, I only had to wait a week to see Jon again. I couldn't remember the last time I'd spent a real weekend with a guy, but I was pretty certain whenever it was, it wasn't as stress-free as my time with Jon. I mean, I had my usual moments of panic, like where and when I would go number two without his ever ever ever suspecting that I had, but other than that I just felt relaxed and happy.

After that weekend, I felt pretty confident that neither of us was interested in dating anyone else, but it seemed a little early for me to think about it and I definitely wasn't going to be the one to bring it up. I appreciated that he was really open with me and didn't try to play it cool, so I was doing the same thing, but there are still some things I am a traditional girl about. I mean, I'll fuck you on the first date but I sure am not going to be the one to bring up "the talk." Boundaries, you guys . . . boundaries.

But one night, soon after that trip, while he and I were texting, the subject just kind of came up when he asked me if I would still be willing to date him when he had to go back to Seattle for work.

"Of course," I replied. "It isn't even that long of a flight from L.A. to Seattle."

"I know, but it might be hard sometimes. After the season starts, it won't be as easy to visit each other for a few months."

Considering that it was March, and the season started in September, I knew that he was looking ahead to the future, and I liked it. After a couple more texts where we both confirmed we were very much interested in seeing where this "thing" could go, he sent me a text that made my tummy jump.

"So you and me?" he wrote.

I paused, smiled, responded. "Yeah, you and me."

And just like that, after five years of barely even having a date, I was in a full-blown relationship.

The next day, I e-mailed Sarah Tilley and told her to go ahead and take that stupid Match.com profile down. As soon as I hit "send" on the e-mail, I held my breath, waiting for her to reply and tell me that this was way too soon, that she had put effort into this and I had agreed to it and *what about the six-pack*?

Instead, I got a very supportive, happy e-mail from her.

"So you're not mad?" I asked her.

"What? No, not at all! You seem really happy and he seems crazy about you. That's all I care about."

"Thank you, that means a lot to me. But I'm sorry you wasted time on Match.com. You can't get those hours back."

"It was fun. Plus, I think the fact that you were so open to meeting someone was because of me."

"Are you fishing for some credit here?"

"No. But you can admit that, right?"

"Yes, you get some credit," I responded. And I actually meant it.

She gave me the password to the account so that I could go and cancel it, plus she figured now that this endeavor was over I should get to see the profile she'd created for me. Below is word for word what the "About Me" section said:

- - -

**W**hat you should know about me . . . I love that show *Bar Rescue* (it's awesome, right?), I hate malls and when I'm sober, I can stay quiet during movies (which is supremely important). Also . . . I am a fiercely loyal person and you will know and feel that if you are in my life. I work hard but know how to enjoy life to the fullest, I see humor in almost everything, I'm passionate, and I'm loyal (I already said that but I am running out of good qualities). At this point in my life, I am not going into dating with a concrete "profile" that I am looking for. I am just really open to meeting and getting to know new, interesting people.

**W**ow, *she knows me really well,* I thought as I read it. *And I really do love* Bar Rescue. If you haven't seen that show, might I suggest a Saturday-afternoon binge-watching marathon? You can thank me later.

I scrolled down to read more about myself. "I like to try new places, not a huge fan of waiting in lines at bars . . . always down for a dive with a good jukebox."

*Huh, all true,* I marveled.

"I exercise five or more times per week."

*Well, I exercise like four times a week, but I'd like to exercise five or more.*

"I like Aerobics, Dancing, Running, Walking/Hiking, Weights/Machines, Yoga."

*Aerobics? Who the fuck still does aerobics?*

The photo she chose as my lead photo was this one:

*I guess she figured it's important a potential suitor knows that I'm flexible.*

And the second photo people saw when they browsed my profile was this:

*No wonder she didn't find me anyone who seemed normal.*

After making fun of Tilley for referencing a workout routine from the 1980s, I hit "delete profile." My reverse-catfishing
days were behind me. At least for now.

For me, one of the challenges of dating someone new is
knowing that they will ultimately see me do stand-up—not
because I don't think I'm good at it; I know I am, and I love
doing it. But, as I've mentioned previously, not everyone is
that comfortable watching their significant other tell stories
to strangers, and that's definitely what I do. I am more of a
storyteller onstage, which means I tell (mostly) true stories,
which means I reveal a lot about myself when I do stand-up.
I'm comfortable with that, but that doesn't mean everyone else
is going to be. Ryan, for instance, never was.

So, just a few weeks into our dating, I had shows in New
York, and Jon asked if he could come.

"Oh, well . . . sure," I said.

"Oh, I don't have to if you don't want me to. It's okay."

"No, I do want you to. It just makes me really nervous. I'm
sorry. But I want you to come."

That's the other thing: I get very nervous about someone
seeing me perform for the first time. That doesn't just go for
dating, it goes for friends, family, coworkers. I'm so much
more at ease in a room full of strangers seeing me for the first
time than I am with anyone I know.

"Well, I'm going to be really nervous the first time you see
me play," he responded. "But I know you're going to see me
play many, many times. And I'm going to see you perform

many, many times. So once we both get the first one out of the way, we'll be fine."

"You're pretty good at this," I wrote back. "See you in New York."

Of all places, I was glad he was coming to New York. It seemed better than having him see me for the first time in some random city in the middle of nowhere, where they put me up at a Hilton Garden Inn and I wake up next to a half-eaten Hot Pocket. No, New York was the best-case scenario. It's a fun city, I have friends there, and I love the club I work in and the hotel where I stay when I'm there.

Before the first show, we went out to dinner and I openly worried about how many people would be in the audience. For the most part, when I perform at clubs now there is always a good crowd.

*But what if? What if for some reason nobody comes to this show? Like not even one person? Could you imagine? Oh my God, what if that happened?*

"You'd think I was such a loser," I told him as I laid out my worst-case scenario for him.

"I would never think that, babe. Never. I would just think that people were stupid for not going."

"You always say the right thing." I smiled.

"But that isn't going to happen. I mean, at least one person will be there . . . me."

I laughed. "I must sound ridiculous. Even when I first started performing, there was never just not anyone there."

"It's going to turn me on to see you perform. I'm already so proud of you."

His words were so sweet and so incredibly supportive that it was hard to still be nervous, but I managed to remain terrified up until the point my foot hit the stage, which is when I always finally breathe.

At first, I felt like I was too in my head knowing that Jon was in the room, and then I was yelling at myself in my head for being in my head. But it turned out to be a great show, with a great crowd. There was totally more than one person there. And at least the first time of Jon seeing me perform was now behind me.

Jon had to start back at work the day after Easter, and I had shows basically every weekend before and after then, so he suggested we go away that week.

"Where do you want to go?" I asked.

"Somewhere warm," he suggested.

"Like Mexico?" I replied.

"Yes! Mexico! All I want to do is lie on a beach and have cocktails and hang out with you."

*Oh my God, he's perfect.*

"So we don't have to go on any hikes or anything?" I wrote back.

"What? NO. That sounds awful."

So, we planned a trip to Playa del Carmen.

"Oh my God! You found the guy to go on a beach vacation with you!" Jackie exclaimed one night over drinks. "Think about it. You've always wanted someone who wanted to do that with you."

She was right. It sounds so simple, but apparently it isn't—at least not for me. And it was the perfect beach vacation. We woke up and went right out to our cabana every day. We had sex in the infinity pool outside our room at night (sorry, I think they drain it when people leave though, right?). We had a romantic dinner alone on the end of a pier that was *his idea*. And once again, it was just easy. The only thing I felt weird or uncomfortable about was the bathroom situation. That's just never going to change.

Our last night in Mexico, as we sat listening to the waves crash and sipping—what else—champagne, we talked about our relationship.

"I know it feels like it happened kind of fast, but it just feels right," he said as I held in a hiccup, because that would have totally ruined the moment. I can't hold my champagne the way he can, okay?

"I agree," I said, smiling, as I felt the hiccup escape my mouth. It was really loud. "Oh my God, how embarrassing," I moaned.

"Oh, stop it. You don't ever have to be embarrassed around me," he said as he pulled me into his arms.

"Ah, thank you."

"But for the record, it was super loud."

"I hate you."

"Well, that sucks because I love you."

So there it was.

"I love you, too." I smiled. And I meant it.

"I had given up on finding someone until I retired," he told me. "It's just so hard with all the traveling."

"Me too!"

"I know, it's like we're perfect together." He smiled.

He was right. I had thought that there was no way I could meet someone when I was constantly on the road for work. It had never occurred to me I might meet someone else, in a totally different profession, who had the same problem. And now here I was, sitting on a beach with a guy who not only understood me but also supported me in what I did.

Once we realized we hadn't had dinner, we wandered into the hotel restaurant to get some food, mostly so that we could keep drinking.

As we walked in, Jon excused himself to use the restroom and I stood next to the hostess stand.

"Table for *uno?*" the hostess asked as she approached.

"Table for *dos,*" I said.

And I'm not going to lie: it felt pretty fucking good.

## Sleeping Single Again

It's one o'clock in the morning and I'm writing this from my bed. I'm under a pile of covers with a pillow propping up my laptop. I have the air-conditioning cranked up because it's currently summer in Southern California. I know that most of the country thinks it's always summer here, which it kind of is, but this is *actual* summer, okay?

What's weird is that when I started my first book, I was in a relationship. By the time I finished it, I was single. I started writing *this* book while I was single and now here I am writing the end of it and I'm in a relationship. There are probably only two people more surprised than me that I found myself finishing this book in a relationship:

1. My editor, as it's definitely not the ending I submitted when I sent out the book proposal months ago.

2. My friend Liz, a.k.a. "Two Rings," who marvels at the fact that my Instagram account went from pictures of wacky signs I see when traveling the country and pictures of me holding my terminally ill cat to pictures of me and my boyfriend, always smiling.

But I kind of like that about this process. While I'm putting my life down on paper, things are changing. That's life, after all, so if I'm going to write about my life I suppose I should be ready for change.

As usual, I'm pretty certain I just heard someone walking around upstairs, but even though I'm finally in an adult relationship, I still have to fend off imaginary intruders on my own, at least for now.

I'm still a big fan of alone time, a big fan of silence, and a big fan of getting to do whatever I want. That being said, I'm not really concerned anymore about someone putting my expensive underwear in the dryer. It's just underwear, after all, and I do have several pairs of them. I mean, I say that now, but I'm sure the first time Jon damages my expensive underwear by throwing them in the dryer, I'm going to have the urge to react poorly. What I hope for myself (and for him) is that I can suppress that urge and not have an irrational argument about how my favorite underwear can now only comfortably fit my dead cat. I believe I'm going to be able to suppress it, as long as I don't have PMS. In that case it won't be my fault and he should have fucking remembered *not to dry the lacy underwear! It isn't that difficult of a request!*

The good thing is, we've had that conversation. Not about underwear in particular, but about the fact that we both have lived alone for quite a while now and we both know it's not going to be easy to learn to share our space with someone again. But for me, the difference between before I met him and now is that I truly look forward to the day I can take on that challenge.

Both of our jobs are going to keep us from being able to live together, or even in the same state, for at least a couple more years, so maybe it's easy for me to say that I'm looking forward to it because there's a pretty solid amount of time before it becomes a reality. But I think what's happening here is that after thirty-nine years, I finally know what I want . . . and what I deserve. Plus, lying next to a big strong football player is going to make those nights when I think I hear footsteps in my house much easier to sleep through, which means I'll be more well rested, which means I'll be much easier to live with. I think.

I still worry more than I should about my future, maybe even more so now because I have someone I plan to share it with. At one point in my life I thought I had found perfect balance, then I fell off the balance beam. Now I'm more realistic: I don't think I've necessarily found *perfect* balance, but I feel more balanced, and that's progress. I'm not positive that total balance and calm is achievable unless you're a monk or Maya Angelou, may she rest in peace, but I am positive that progress is progress and as long as I'm growing and learning, everything is going to be fine. Or even, dare I say . . . amazing.

There's always a possibility, too, that by the time you read this book, my relationship will have somehow crumbled or ended in a fight over ruined expensive underwear. I've learned that things don't always turn out how you expect them to. But I've also learned that this isn't always a negative—sometimes they turn out even better than expected.

What I know for certain is that I found someone who loves me for me, and I love him for him, which ultimately is what we all deserve. Also, I'm really thankful for Twitter.

Gotta go, I just heard something upstairs.

## Acknowledgments

I want to thank and acknowledge the following people:

My parents, Eric and Cheryl Henderson and Jim and Shirley Colonna, for always believing in and supporting me, even when they probably just wish I'd be a little less honest.

Jennifer Colonna-Quinton, for being such a good, supportive big sister.

My nephew, Nicholas. At sixteen years old, you're already the kind of man most only aspire to be.

My book agent, Robert Guinsler. You're the best.

Jen Bergstrom, Kate Dresser, and Tricia Boczkowski at Gallery Books for making this happen.

Abbey MacDonald and Lindsay Howard . . . you know why.

Everyone who represents me at APA and New Wave, who fight for my career on a daily basis. I appreciate the time you put into this more than you know.

Jeff Cohen.

Nelly Gonzalez for making me feel pretty even when I was pantsless.

Lisa Perkins and Alex Martinetti.

Blake Little and John Vairo for figuring out how to translate what was in my brain into a book cover.

All of my friends—thank you. I love you and you make my life better. Also, thank you for letting me talk about you.

All of the Morgans and Colonnas, and Leanne McClintock and Victoria Ishmael, for being the family I can always count on.

And Jonathan Ryan, for finally showing me what it's like to be loved for who you are.